FIX YOUR PROBLEMS
– The Tenali Raman's Way

Vishal Goyal

PUSTAK MAHAL

Publishers
Pustak Mahal®
J-3/16, Daryaganj, New Delhi-110002
☎ 23276539, 23272783, 23272784 • Fax: 011-23260518
E-mail: info@pustakmahal.com • Website: www.pustakmahal.com

Sales Centre
- 10-B, Netaji Subhash Marg, Daryaganj, New Delhi-110002
  ☎ 23268292, 23268293, 23279900 • Fax: 011-23280567
  E-mail: rapidexdelhi@indiatimes.com
- Hind Pustak Bhawan
  6686, Khari Baoli, Delhi-110006
  ☎ 23944314, 23911979

Branches
Bengaluru: ☎ 080-22234025 • Telefax: 080-22240209
E-mail: pustak@airtelmail.in • pustak@sancharnet.in
Mumbai: ☎ 022-22010941, 022-22053387
E-mail: rapidex@bom5.vsnl.net.in
Patna: ☎ 0612-3294193 • Telefax: 0612-2302719
E-mail: rapidexptn@rediffmail.com
Hyderabad: Telefax: 040-24737290
E-mail: pustakmahalhyd@yahoo.co.in

© **Pustak Mahal, New Delhi**

ISBN 978-81-223-1127-3

Edition: 2010

The Copyright of this book, as well as all matter contained herein (including illustrations) rests with the Publishers. No person shall copy the name of the book, its title design, matter and illustrations in any form and in any language, totally or partially or in any distorted form. Anybody doing so shall face legal action and will be responsible for damages.

Printed at : Param Offsetters, Okhla, New Delhi-110020

Dedication

To
My mother and father
The light house of inspiration and morality

Acknowledgements

$\mathcal{F}$or me, 'Fix Your Problems – The Tenali Raman's Way' is a dream come true. Now that my dream has taken shape, I want to acknowledge the precious support and strength I received from all those who rejuvenated my mental faculty to serve up this book with the right recipe, the right ingredients and the right flavour that suits the palate of every reader. Among the many people who helped me with this book, my special thanks to my parents for encouraging me and showing keen interest in the progress, to both my elder brothers and sister-in-laws for philosophical discussions, to my wife who listened to the contents, and to my toddler son Aryan and my nephews who at their tender age, have sacrificed many hours which we could have spent together.

I am grateful to my senior colleague Sh. G.S.Bains, Chief Manager, PSWC, from whom I silently drew inspiration.

I am also grateful to Shri Ram Avtar Gupta, the Chairman of **Pustak Mahal** for having great confidence in me and for rekindling my passion. I have truly found a mentor in him and to Shri S.K. Roy, the Executive Editor, for taking care of me during the initial legwork and in giving the final shape to this book with beautiful illustrations and pleasing cover which in itself speaks a lot, and the entire production team for supporting me to the fullest.

My special thanks go to Shri Walter Vieira, a profound Management Guru and a practitioner of management discipline, who very selectively helped to suggest the key lessons and morals at the end of each anecdote.

Finally, I would like to thank that all of them who knowingly or unknowingly have contributed to this book.

Vishal Goyal
Chandigarh, 1st February'2010

Reverence To Raman
(*A Prospective*)

$\mathcal{N}$ow onwards, this book will aptly narrate some of the selectively collected popular stories about the life style, combination and co-ordination of King Krishnadeva Raya and Tenali Raman in and out of the Imperial Court. These stories enlighten, advice, motivate, encourage, entertain and spread the message of intellect, time-tuning, and strategic stroking besides having a lip smacking flavour of lively wit and humour that can be precisely applied to all ordeals, trials and problems in context to every day life. Apart from this, each story of this wordly-wise man of yesterday **Tenali Raman** contains a deep meaning and has a lesson ingrained into it which needs to be assimilated by every reader for his personal growth and development.

Though, it is a herculean task to define the personality of a character of the stature of Tenali Raman, However, a brief functional resume of Tenali Raman can be attempted to portray the qualities and traits possessed by him, which can be imbibed by anyone.

Personal Profile

Name: Garlapati Tenali Ramakrishna popularly known as Tenali Raman or Tenali Ramalinga.

Family Background:

• A Brahmin who lived during early 16th century A.D.

• Originally hailed from Tumuluru village near the coastal town of Tenali (Guntur District of present day Andhra Pradesh).

Employment Profile

One of the eight poets called the 'ashtadiggajas' (the eight elephants serving as pillars) of King Krishadeva Raya's Royal Court – the Bhuvana Vijayam (Global Victor).

Tuluva Sri Krishna deva Raya (1509-1529 CE) [a.k.a Krishna Raya; Kannada Rajya Rama Ramana; Mooru Rayara Ganda and Andhra Bhoja], was the famed Emperor of Vijayanagara Empire (modern day Karnataka State) who devolved a 'Golden Era'.

Profile of Qualities

- Great scholar of several languages (including Marathi, Tamil, Kannada, Telugu and Sanskrit)
- Poet of knowledge, acute wit, intelligence, shrewdness and ingenuity.
- Intelligent advisor to King Raya.

Special Skills

Tenali Raman was a witty and intellectual person who adorned the Royal Court of King Raya. Tenali possessed all the Critical Success Factors (C.S.Fs) to win and sustain competitive advantage. He judiciously adopted the 'F.A.C.T.S.' strategy for an effective recognition programme in and out of the Imperial Court. This 'F.A.C.T.S.' strategy is understood to simply contain traits as:

- Fairness to achieve high performance;
- Appropriateness to enhance tacit (implied) knowledge;
- Consistency to think and act;
- Timeliness to establish parameters;
- Sincerity towards the State (Country).

General Profile

He wrote some of the greatest poetic works and devotional texts such as:

- Udbhataradhya Charitramu (based on the story of Udbhatta, a monk)
- Panduranga Mahatmyamu (one among the Panch Kavyas) and
- Ghatikachala Mahatmyamu (on Ghatikachalam, a place of worship for God Narasimha near Vellore).

TITLES:

Stern and sarcastic in his wit and instrumental in protecting King Raya's prestige many times by coming to his rescue in critical situations, that Tenali Raman earned himself titles such as

- Vikata Kavi (clown-jester-poet);
- Kumara Bharathi; and
- Andhra Paris.

These traits can be easily understood by a close analysis of the following acronym which corresponds to the name of this great witty character –T.E.N.A.L.I. - R.A.M.A.N:

1. Talent development through leveraging resources and achieving 'strategic fit'.
2. Effective collaboration of different types of knowledge, wit and humor.
3. Nurture open, honest and effective communication.
4. Accumulating resources through mining experience in order to achieve faster leaning and capabilities.
5. Leadership qualities to be displayed in all crucial circumstances. Leadership is a guiding vision involving self knowledge, candour and maturity. Leadership is daring, is curiosity and is a passion to achieve results.
6. Inspiring a shared vision to practice visible Management.
7. Realistic focus on extrinsic as well as intrinsic vision.
8. Align S.M.A.R.T. objectives for the Kingdom (Country) and individual aspirations for promoting mutual benefits.
9. Modelling the way enabling others to act.
10. Appraise personal performance to embed vision.
11. Need to control everything very carefully.

Ofcourse, in this technology driven era, Tenali Raman can be described as guru of all gurus which make us immediately remind of what John. F. Kennedy once said, "Man is still the most extraordinary computer of all".

Contents

Prologue 10

1. The Sunrise 17
2. The Prodigy 21
3. Rendezvous with King Raya 23
4. The Last Riddle 26
5. Food Facts 28
6. Point Blank 30
7. Holy Mess 32
8. The Arithmetic of Age 34
9. The Master of Game 37
10. Piece to peace 40
11. Code of Brilliance 42
12. Spectacular Water 45
13. A Bonafide Verdict 47
14. A perfect Lesson 50
15. A Calculated Act 53
16. The Slippery Travellers 55
17. Guessing Game 57
18. Nine of Ten 61
19. Blinded by Lure 64
20. A Dauntless Act 66
21. Grain Gain 69
22. Joy in the City of Joy 72
23. Flight of the Imagination 76
24. An Eye Opener 79
25. Master Stroke 82
26. The Grand Plan 84
27. The Knotty Knot 87
28. The Desert Taster 90
29 Measure for Measure 93
30. Pursuit for Justice 96
31. The Final Solution 99
32. The Master's Move 101
33. Dog's Trail 103
34. Your Honour's Honour Honoured 105
35. Wicked Word 108

36. The Blamesworthy 111

37. Windfall Deal 114

38. The Wish List 117

39. The Striking
    Questions 120

40. An Ugly Truth 123

41. Twinkle in Wrinkle 126

42. The Son'Shine 129

43. The Rich versus
    the Poor 133

44. Cup of Woes 136

45. Of the People, For the
    People, By the People 138

46. Search Simplified 140

47. A Landmark Victory 144

48. Under Cover 147

49. Dons to Dust 150

50. The Phoenix Moment 154

51. Acting Care-fooly 156

52. The Bold One 159

53. Wanted: An Urgent
    Solution 161

54. Testing Times 164

55. Winner All the Way 167

56. A Special Encounter 170

57. Prize Catch 174

58. Lost and Found 177

59. Left High and Dry 179

60. Meeting of Minds 182

61. Intelligent Strikes 185

62. Yours is Here 188

63. Who's Who 190

64. There it goes, again 194

65 The Namesake 196

66. A Tactful Move 198

67. Bare in Mind 201

68. Battle of Wits 204

69. Hand'some Win 207

70. Scene by Scene 209

71. Next is What 212

72. Handle with Care 216

73. Discovery Lesson 219

74. Adieu to Raman 222

Prologue

*I*ndia is the world's most ancient civilization and a land of manifold interests. India is so extensive that other countries are not equal a hundredth part of it. All of us, who wear cotton cloth, use the decimal system, enjoy the taste of chicken, play chess or roll dice, love mangoes and elephants, and seek peace of mind, tranquility or good health by standing on our heads or through meditation feel indebted to India.

Ancient wisdom enshrined in the Vedas, Upanishads, Smritis, Sudras, Dharamshastras and the witty folklore witnessed during the mighty ruling dynasties, is the chief solvent of old ideas in India and infact the chief source from which new ones are generated. This voluntary character of the thoughts and feelings of the people who made the unique Indian social, political and economic fabric down the ages, needs to be strikingly illuminated not only to each of the millions of Indians but amongst the world populace.

Sailing, say to India, from Britain down through the Atlantic, close by the coast of Portugal and Spain, and then, within the Mediterranean, skirting the coast of Algeria, and so on, one can see the land inhabited by human beings displaying peculiar and impeccable signs of life and the tragedies and comedies that are daily being enacted by the humane Indians in their homes, that constantly generates unmatched wisdom.

The ineffable fascination of modern India is a product of the complexity of its many ages of coexistent reality. Nothing is ever totally forgotten in this land of reincarnation. Paradoxically, the so-called Westerners' assertion of cultural superiority define everything

Rendezvous with
King Raya

The Vijayanagar Empire had a prominent place in the pre-independent deccan India. King Sri Krishnadeva Rāya, among the rulers of Vijayanagar Kingdom, transformed his regime into a golden era.

Garlapati Tenāli Ramakrishna popularly known as Tenāli Raman, the simple Brahmin and scholarly poet from Tumuluru near Tenāli fell upon such hard times that he was no longer able to feed his family. Hearing that King Rāya greatly encouraged talent and was famed for his generosity, Tenāli set off for the Royal Palace in Hampi.

When brought before the King in the Bhuvana Vijayam, (Global Victor, the Royal Court), he bowed low. The King asked him to recite a poem. On hearing his recitation, the King, well-pleased, asked him to name his reward.

"State-of-art, straight from the heart"

Tenāli, pointing to a finely wrought chess board lying before the King said, "Your Highness, if you place just one grain of rice on the first square of this chessboard and double it for every square, I will consider myself well-rewarded."

"Are you sure?" asked the King, greatly surprised, "Just grains of rice, not gold?"

"Yes, Your Highness," affirmed the humble poet.

"So it shall be," ordered the King and his courtiers started placing the grain on the chessboard. One grain on the first square, 2 on the second, 4 on the third, 8 on the fourth, 16 on the fifth and so on. By the time they came to the 10th square, they had to place 512 grains of rice. The number swelled to 5,24,288 grains on the 20th square. When they came to the halfway mark, the 32nd square, the grain count was 214,74,83,648; that is over 214 crores! Soon the count increased to lakhs of crores.

Everybody in the court was awestruck and eventually a situation came when King Rāya was left with no other option than to handover his entire granary to the clever poet.

Just at that moment, Tenāli interrupted and said, "O King, I do not want anything either from you or your Kingdom. This was just a lesson to teach the importance of small steps which compound to big victories. I also want Your Honour to make progress in the same manner in all his endeavours."

Hearing this, King Rāya was greatly pleased with Tenāli Raman who made him understand the power of compounding which began with just one grain of rice! King Rāya not only inducted Tenāli Raman as his ashtadiggajas (Eight strong pillars) of the Bhuvana Vijayam (Global Victor) but relied on Tenāli's resourcefulness of knowledge, immense wit and intelligence, shrewdness and ingenuity.

Tenāli Raman, thereafter, shone among the eight ashtadiggajas as a precious gem in the diamond-studded crown.

of India as mystical, unscientific, traditional, group-oriented, other-worldly, and autocratic and identify themselves superior in all endeavours. This deep-rooted prejudice about the qualities, traditions and religions of India has been pervasive and marked characteristic of Western thought in recent centuries who totally forget the rich ancient culture and valour of India and the intellectuals such as Birbal , Chanakya , Manu, Tenali Raman , and similar breed that proliferated in India and adorned the palaces of some of the mightiest rulers of the Indian soil.

For this reason, it is foolish to maintain the inertia of blind modernism and shut one's eyes to these pleasant facts about India's historic grandeur and to hide it from the public. Here, in the present book, an effort is made to discuss one such imperial character that prevailed during the 16th century A.D. in the Vijayanagara Empire down the Southern India.

The Vijayanagara Empire also referred as the Kingdom of Bisnaga by the Portuguese, was a South Indian Empire based in the Deccan Plateau. The city was built around the original religious centre of the Virupksha temple at Hampi. Vijayanagara now stands as a ruined city in Bellary District, northern Karnataka. As the prosperous capital of the largest and the most powerful kingdom of its time in all of India, Vijayanagara still attracts people from all round the world. The ruined city is a UNESCO World Heritage site (where it is called the 'Ruins of Hampi'). In recent years, there have been concerns regarding damage to the site at Hampi from heavy vehicular traffic and the construction of road bridges in the vicinity. Hampi is now listed as a "threatened" World Heritage Site, and is included in the 'UNESCO List of World Heritage in Danger:1999'.

It is widely believed that Vijayanagara was the largest city in India and the 2nd largest in the world at the end of the 15th century with 5,00,000 inhabitants. The city flourished between the 14th century and the 16th century, during the height of the power of the Vijayanagara Empire. During this time, the empire was often in conflict with the Muslim Kingdoms which had become established in the Northern Deccan, and which were often collectively termed the Deccan Sultanates.

When the mighty sultans of Delhi – Alla-ud-din-Khilji and Muhammad bin Tughlaq repeatedly invaded the Deccan Hindu Kingdoms, two hindu princes popularly called the Sangama brothers --- Hakka (Harihara) and Bukka Raya founded an independent Kingdom known as the 'Vijayanagara Empire' in the region between the rivers Krishna and Tungabhadra during 1336 in order to check the progress of Islam in the South. Hakka and Bukka were sons of Sangama -- one of the chiefs at the Court of the Hoysala ruler.

Hakka became the first ruler of the Vijayanagara Kingdom and after his death, his brother Bukka Raya succeeded. The successive rulers of the Vijayanagara Empire caused decades of conflicts, invasions, annexations and internal rebellions which resulted the Vijayananagra dynasty to decline during the late 15th century until serious attempts were made by commander Saluva Narasimha Devaraya during 1485 and by general Tuluva Narasa Nayaka during 1491 to reconsolidate the Empire. After nearly two decades of conflict with rebellious chieftains, the Empire eventually came under the rule of Tuluva Sri Krishnadevaraya , son of an army commander Tuluva Narasa Nayaka and Nagala Devi.

In the following decades, Vijayanagara empire dominated all of southern India and reached its peak during the rule of Krishnadevaraya when the Vijayanagara armies were consistently victorious. The empire annexed areas formerly under the Sultanates in northern deccan and territories in the eastern deccan, including Kalinga, while maintaining control over all its subordinates in south India. Krishnadeva's rule was of long sieges, bloody conquests, and victories through relentless clashes with the constant threats of the Gajapatis of Orissa, the Bahamani Sultans, the feudatory chiefs of Ummatur, Reddys of Kondavidu, Velamas of Bhuvanagiri and invasions of Bidar, Gulbarga, Golconda, Kovilkonda and Bijapur.

Krishnadeva Raya (1509-1529) was one of the great emperors of India who also earned the titles of Kannada Rajya Rama Ramana; Mooru Rayara Ganda (meaning King of three kings) and Andhra Bhoja. King

Raya was not only an able administrator, but also an excellent army general who presided over the empire at its zenith and is regarded as an icon by all Indians and especially the Tuluvas, Kannadigas amd Telugus.

The empire went into slow decline regionally after King Raya. The rule of Krishnadeva Raya is a glorious chapter in Vijayanagara history when its armies were successful everywhere. It was a 'Golden Era'. King Raya is still considered par excellence to Ashoka, Samudra Gupta and Harsha Vardhana. Recently on 27th to 29th Janaury'2010, the Government of Karnataka celebrated the 500th year of coronation of this great emperor under whose rule, the pomp and gaiety of the Vijayanagara empire reached its zenith.

The writings of medieval European travelers such as Domingo Paes, Fernao Nuniz and Niccolo Da Conti, the literature in local vernaculars and archeological excavations reveal the empire's power and wealth. The empire's patronage enabled fine arts and literature to reach new heights and the empire created an epoch in south Indian history that transcended regionalism, by promoting Hinduism as a unifying factor. The rule of Krishnadeva Raya was an age of prolific literature in many languages. Numerous Telugu, Sanskrit, Kannada and Tamil poets enjoyed the patronage of the emperor. Eight poets known as Ashtadiggajalu or ashtadiggajas (eight elephants in the eight cardinal points such as North, South and so on) were part of his Imperial Court (known as Bhuvana Vijayam). According to the Vaishnavite religion, there are eight elephants in eight corners in space and hold the earth in its place. Similarly, these poets were the eight pillars of his literary assembly and it is popularly believed to include – Allasani Peddana (honoured with the title of father of Telugu poetry), Nandi Thimmana, Madayyagiri Mallana, Dhurjati, Ayyala-raju-Rama Bhadrudu, Pingali Surana, Rama Raj Bhushanudu and Tenali Ramakrishna. Although the ashtadiggajas were regarded as the pillars of the literary assembly, Tenali Raman remains one of the most popular figures in India today, a quick witted courtier ready even to outwit the all powerful emperor.

Garlapati Tenali Ramakrishna popularly known as Tenali Raman and Tenali Ramalinga was a Brahmin who originally hailed from Tumuluru village near the coastal town of Thenali (Guntur District of present day Andhra Pradesh). A devotee of goddess Kali, Tenali Raman became the court jester of King Raya with his wit and intelligence and shined among the ashtadiggajas and other courtiers as a precious gem in the diamond studded crown. Tenali Raman added feathers to the crown of reputation of King Krishnadeva Raya. Tenali became instrumental in protecting the emperor's prestige many times by coming to his rescue in critical situations.

Tenali Raman was a populist philosopher and a wise man, remembered to this day for his stories and anecdotes laced with wit and intelligence. The anecdotes attributed to Tenali Raman reveal a satirical personality with a biting tongue that Tenali was not afraid to use even against the most tyrannical rulers (the Delhi Sultans) of his time. The anecdotes were used to express certain ideas by Tenali, allowing the bypassing of the normal discriminative thought patterns.

This book is a wealth of concise, useable, quote-worthy wit and wisdom revealed by the stories, toasts, snippets and anecdotes of Tenali Raman whether in King Raya's Royal Court or in the civilian life of the Vijayanagara Empire , that lie, waiting to be used, on every page. Much of Tenali's actions can vividly be described as bizarre yet normal, simple yet profound, natural yet sharp, straight yet logical, and prompt yet rational. What adds even further to his uniqueness is the way, Tenali got across his messages and the uncanny situations in unconventional yet very effective methods in a profound simplicity. The book brings together a broad range of items and verses on common themes, providing the readers with an overview of thinking how to overcome the everyday precarious situations. This arrangement of fables impregnated with several 'layers' of meaning allows you to find those perfectly appropriate motivational ways to beat a given scary situation. These fables purvey a pithy fold wisdom that triumphs overall trials and tribulations. Perhaps, here Oscar Wilde's 1892 comment can inspire a demoralized and defeated reader: "We are all in the gutter, but some of us are looking at the stars." Paging through **"Tenali Raman"**, you'll find yourself armed with abundant supply of distilled thought stockpiled in front of you. The tales of Tenali deal with concepts that have certain timelessness. The themes in the tales have become part of the folklore that is found to fit almost any occasion. Superficially, most of the Tenali stories may be told as humorous anecdotes, yet they are engrossed with management maxims and lessons which are favourably told and retold endlessly in the teahouses of Southern India and can still in heard in homes and educational institutes. But it is inherent in a Tenali story that it may be understood at many levels. There is an anecdote, followed by a management lesson or moral – and usually the little extra which brings the consciousness of the potential mystic a little further on the way to realization. You're bound to find that snippet of inspiration that objectifies the thinking process or snappy comeback you need to win your own personal skirmishes.

So don't forget that as, Sir Francis Bacon wrote in 1597, "Knowledge is power." Turn the page and become empowered.

LIFE'S LESSON

"Many times we look, but do not see. We hear but do not listen. We cannot imagine that great complexity can be cloaked by simplicity. The razor blade appears straight and sharp, until put under a microscope wherein the edge appears to be fogged!"

Wise Cracks

- ☼ Progress is the law of life.
- ☼ Progress is not an accident but a necessity; it is a part of nature.
- ☼ Progress is the activity of today and assurance of tomorrow.
- ☼ To progress gradually in steps makes the individuals outgrow institutions, as children outgrow clothes.

Quotable Nuggets

"Nature knows no pause in progress and development."

J.W. Goethe

The
Last Riddle

When Thodsam Chandu, a rich landowner of Ummatur and a close friend of Tenāli Raman was on his deathbed gasping for breath, he called for his three sons. Chandu told his sons to dig under his bed when he breathes his last. Saying that, he breathed his last.

Few days later, all three dug the spot and unearthed three pots placed one above the other. The topmost pot contained mud; the middle pot contained dried cow dung and the lowest pot contained straw. Below this pot, there was a small purse containing ten varahas (gold coins).

On seeing this, the siblings were baffled.

"Obviously, our father meant to convey some deep message to us through the pots and their contents," said the eldest brother, "but what?"

They wracked their brains but none of them could come up with a satisfactory explanation. Finally, they decided to consult Tenāli Raman who was their family friend.

"A balancing act"

When all three reached Tenāli's place and narrated the occurrence, Tenāli laughed at the problem put before him.

"Your father was an intellectual person who loved puzzles," he said, "I think he could not resist in putting a last one. The interpretation to this problem is simple. The topmost pot contains mud, you say. That means he wants his eldest son to have his fields. The second pot contains dried cow dung. It means he wants his second son to have his herd of cattle. The last pot contains straw, you say. Now straw is golden-coloured. That means, he wants his youngest son to have all his gold."

The brothers were happy with the way their father had apportioned his wealth and marvelled at Tenāli's sagacity.

"But one thing remains unexplained," said the youngest brother. "What about the varahas lying in the purse at the bottom of pots?" he continued to question.

"Your father was a bright person who kept everybody contended and happy. He knew you would come to consult me," smiled Tenāli. "The coins are my fee," he said laughingly pocketing the coins.

Life's Lesson

"Having solved the problem satisfactorily, Tenali was not going to have the three brothers quarelling over ten gold coins. Therein lies the wisdom of greats, quick and fair thinkers like Solomon and Tenali."

Wise Cracks

☼ An effective person continues to communicate, negotiate and teach lessons and distribute resources watchfully by calculating all risks and oppositions, and in the process keeping everybody contended.

Quotable Nuggets

"Logical consequences are the scarecrows of fools and the beacons of wise men."

T.H. Huxley

Food Facts

Once King Krishnadeva Rāya got badly affected by chronic cough. As he was in the habit of eating sour things: sour curd, sour buttermilk and pickles etc., the problem worsened. The royal physicians advised the King to give up his habit of eating sour things so that the medicine could be useful to him, but all in vain.

At last the royal physicians approached the court jester Tenāli Raman and explained the deteriorating health of their dear King. Tenāli assured the physicians of finding some solution to the problem.

Next day, Tenāli visited the Royal Court and told the King that he had recently visited a renowned physician in Bellamakonda and discussed the King's habitual cough. Tenāli further told him that while advising a remedy for the disease, the physician has permitted him to eat whatever he liked, including sour things along with his (physician's) prescription.

"United troubles for the king"

Explaining this, Tenāli gave the King the physician's medicine. The King continued with his usual habit of eating sour things. After a few days, when Tenāli enquired about his health, the King said, "The cough has not worsened but neither I have been cured of it."

Tenāli said, "You continue taking the medicine along with sour things. Any person who takes this medicine along with sour things shall surely have three benefits from it."

"Which ones?" asked the King patiently.

Tenāli said, "First, there will be no theft in the house of such a person who takes the medicine along with sour things. Second, no dog will ever bite him. Third, such person will never see old age."

"These are good things, but how the eating of sour things will ensure these three things?" asked the King.

Tenāli said, "If a person goes on eating sour things, he will never be cured of his cough. He will cough day and night, then how can a thief enter his house. The cough will eventually weaken the person and he won't be able to walk without the help of a stick. The stick in hand will ward off dogs, so no dog will bite. Similarly, weakness and disease will kill the person in his youth, hence no old age."

Listening to this, the King understood Tenāli's clever device of advising him to get rid of his gruelling habit of eating sour things. Soon, the King gave up the habit and regained his health.

Wise Cracks

☼ No man can be saved without 'self-control' and 'self-discipline'.

He is the most powerful who has control on his own self. No man is free who can't command himself.

Quotable Nuggets

"Atma Sanyam and Indriya Riproha, control over self and senses, are needed for health and happiness."

Yoga Sutra

"It is better to have self-control than to control an army."

The Bible

Point
Blank

"Why doesn't hair grow on the palms of hands? It's strange but I can't understand this mystery yet!" enquired King Krishnadeva Rāya from his favourite Tenāli Raman one fine day in the Bhuvana Vijayam.

"My Lord! You don't have hair on your palms because your hands are always busy in the generous act of giving donations and gifts to the poor and needy people. The continuous rubbing caused by such kind act of yours is responsible for your palms not having any hair," Tenāli replied smilingly.

The King felt very pleased with Tenāli's reply. King Rāya immediately asked Tenāli, "If this is the reason, then why don't your palms have any hair?"

"O King, as my hands regularly receive rewards and donations from you . . . the rubbing caused from the receipt of such gifts and donations is responsible for my palms having no hair . . . " Tenāli continued to explain.

"Unravelling of a less known secret."

"Still there is no hair on the palms of our other courtiers! Why so . . . ?" enquired King Rāya.

"Your Majesty! When you are kind enough to regularly give donations and gifts to me and others, the envious courtiers intolerantly rub their hands against each other in jealousy. Due to this friction caused by rubbing, there is no hair on their palms!" replied Tenāli Raman.

Tenāli Raman's reply pleased the King but embarrassed the resentful courtiers.

Life's Lesson

"Quick-wit and quick thinking are abilities given to people like Tenali Raman and Birbal. Therefore, they are rightly labelled 'wise men'. They have the wisdom to 'see the world in a grain of sand'. All of us can aspire to do likewise. The glory is in the string."

Wise Cracks

- ☼ No man is a complete failure until he begins disliking men who succeed.
- ☼ Envy (jealousy) is almost the only vice which is practised all the times at every place.
- ☼ He, who envies, admits his inferiority.
- ☼ As iron is eaten by rust, so are the envious consumed by envy.
- ☼ Few men have the strength to honour a friend's success without envy.
- ☼ To honour and to praise makes good men better and bad men worse.

Quotable Nugget

"When the grass looks greener on the other side of the fence, it may be that they take better care of it over there."

Anonymous

Holy
Mess

Once a sage happened to visit a village located on the outskirts of Hampi. The sage performed miracles and delivered religious discourses which pleased the superstitious villagers enormously.

Everyday from morning till late evening, scores of villagers swarmed the temple to listen to the sermons of the sage and offer him gifts and delicacies.

When Tenāli Raman came to learn about the sage, he became suspicious of the sage's conduct.

Later that day, Tenāli went to the temple and sat near the sage along with other villagers. The sage was seated on a slightly elevated platform. He began reciting holy hymns. To Tenāli's utter surprise, the sage went on repeating the same shloka over and over again.

Tenāli became sure that the sage was infact a cheat and was deceiving the innocent villagers by posing as a scholarly saint. Unexpectedly, Tenāli leaned forward towards the sage and plucked a strand of hair from his white beard and screamed victoriously, "I am the lucky one to have the key to the Heaven! I shall gain entry to the Heaven!"

Seeing Tenāli, the villagers looked at him shocked.

"This sage is not an ordinary person but is the greatest and the most intellectual saint of the world. He is so great that if I keep a strand of hair from his beard with me, I will be blessed forever!" said Tenāli showing the strand of hair to the villagers.

Listening to Tenāli's comments, soon there was a commotion amongst the villagers who rushed uncontrollably to get hold of the hair from the sage's beard. Everyone pounced at the sage to have a strand of hair from his beard.

This frightened the deceitful sage so much that he ran for his life and was never heard of again.

Life's Lesson

"The surest way to make an enemy is to say, 'you are wrong'." This technique never fails. Most of us do this and create many enemies. It requires 'wisdom' to use the hand of criticism to gain a 'compliment'.

Wise Cracks

- ☼ Falsehood is so easy, truth is so difficult.
- ☼ It is the act of a bad man to deceive others by falsehood.
- ☼ Tricks and treachery are the practices of fools who don't have brains enough to be honest.
- ☼ He, who keeps back the truth or withholds it from men, is either a coward or a criminal, or both.
- ☼ Keep truth on your side, as it alone is safe and nothing else is safe.

Quotable Nugget

"Satyam vadet, priyam vadet; speak the truth sweetly."

Niti Vakya

"It is twice the pleasure to deceive the deceiver."

Jean De La Fontaine

The Arithmetic of Age

$\mathcal{T}$he affairs of Vijayanagara Empire with Portugal grew so gracious under the regime of King Krishnadeva Rāya that a Portuguese traveller named Domingo Paes even visited Vijayanagara to observe its grandeur. This traveller spent significant periods in the Bhuvana Vijayam (Royal Court of Global victor) and even gave a vivid account of his visit.

Once an affluent Portuguese lady desirous of visiting the architectural marvels of Lord Venkateshwara, Virupaksha and Vithalaswamy temples accompanied Domingo Paes to the imperial capital city of Hampi. When the King was apprised of this, he invited Domingo Paes and the lady to the majestic palace for a lunch. The King was informed that the Portuguese lady spent a lot of time and money on her makeup and was an egoistic lady who liked people admiring her.

"Dialogue to remember for centuries."

Just before the lady visited the royal palace, the King cautioned all his courtiers to be extra careful while conversing or responding to the lady.

The lady was given an affectionate reception and admired the courteousness extended by the King. Soon after the lunch, the King and the lady conversed. During the tete-a-tete, the lady asked the King, "What do you think is my age?"

The King was perplexed to hear such a question and looked at the lady for sometime. He knew that it was difficult to answer the lady and to keep her blissful. However, the King said, "You are an elegant lady and it's very difficult for anybody to precisely arrive at your age. It requires a rational person to guess your age. Only my witty courtier Tenāli Raman is capable of answering you."

Sighting the King to be in a shaky position, Tenāli took control of the situation and said, "Madam, if I consider your dazzling teeth, your age should be 19; but from your wavy brown hair, you can be placed around 18. But if I consider your gentle complexion, you can be said to be no more than 16."

The lady felt extremely flattered at this idea of her age and insisted, "Thank you for your kind opinion, but please do tell me what you consider to be my age?"

"Ma'am, I have already given you my estimate of your age. As I am too weak in calculations, you just have to add 19, 18 and 16 and you will arrive at my guess of your age," replied Tenāli and gave her a broad smile!

The lady was so amazed to hear such an intelligent reply from Tenāli that she suddenly burst into laughter. The King joined her.

Life's Lesson

"How do you say something unpleasent, without being unpleasant? The sting of a bee tells you that spring is here. But the brush of a butterfly's wings makes the same announcement, without a sting. Tact lubricates human interaction. Tact consists of knowing how far you can go!"

Wise Cracks

☼ Tact is an important practical virtue. It is the ability of making a point without making an enemy.

☼ The sting of a bee is a convincing argument that 'spring' has arrived, but the brush of a butterfly's wing tells the same story in a more pleasant manner. Tact is the interpreter of all riddles, the surmounter of all difficulties and remover of all obstacles. Without tact, one can learn nothing.

Quotable Nugget

"Tact is an art of putting it nicely but not precisely."

Anonymous

✲✲✲

The Master of The Game

*W*hen Tenāli Raman shifted to a new house located on a small side street in Hampi, he was faced with an arduous task of putting up with the nuisance of the neighbourhood boys playing noisy games outside his house till late at night.

One evening, when the boys were particularly noisy playing ingorchap (a game which involves hitting a pile of stones with a ball), Tenāli went out to talk with the boys.

Tenāli explained that he was a poet who was happiest when he could see or hear young boys playing his favourite games of korpamguddi (a game which involves locating persons blind-folded), chirra gonne (*gilli danda*), chedugudu (*kabaddi*) and ingorchap. Tenāli told the boys that he felt nostalgic seeing these

"*The street warrior*"

games being played which reminded him of his cheerful and carefree childhood days. Tenāli further told the boys that he would give them ten varahas (gold coins) each week to play these games in the street at night.

The boys were thrilled at this suggestion of Tenāli. They were being paid to do something they enjoyed!

All along the week, the boys played the games till late night. At the end of the first week, the boys knocked at Tenāli's house and asked to be paid.

Tenāli blissfully did so.

The boys continued to play the next week also. At the end of the second week, when they asked for the payment, Tenāli told the boys that he had run out of money and sent the boys away with only seven varahas.

The third week, Tenāli told the boys that he had not yet received payments from his master and gave them only five varahas.

The boys felt disappointed but there was not much they could do about it.

The fourth week Tenāli told the boys that he could not further afford to pay them ten varahas as he had promised, but would anyhow give them two varahas each week without fail.

This was too much for the boys. "You expect us to play seven days a week for a measly two varahas!" they yelled, "go to blazes."

The boys stormed away and never played on the street ever again. Tenāli Raman felt happy at his idea which relieved him of the nuisance of boys and lived happily in his new house.

Life's Lesson

"In everything you do, have a plan. A short-term plan and a long-term plan, have a plan even if you are travelling from one part of the city to another. As the chinese say, 'If you don't know where you are going, any road will take you there.' Where? Anywhere. But wise men like TR know!"

Wise Cracks

- ☼ When pleasure and happiness are used as a business pursuit for earning money, both pleasure and money are lost.
- ☼ Excessive, selfish and greedy love of money is the root of all evil.
- ☼ Money should not make people blind to differentiate pleasure from business.

Quotable Nugget

"He that is of the opinion money will do everything may well be suspected of doing everything, for money."

Proverb

Piece
To Peace

$\mathcal{V}$asu Rao, Tenāli Raman's tightfisted friend always wished his small, noisy house to be larger and quieter without spending much.

One day, in order to get his problem solved, he went straight to Tenāli and explained his need. Tenāli said, "I can solve your problem. Just do as I say."

Without any fuss, Vasu Rao agreed.

"Vasu! If you have some chicks, some sheep, a horse, a pig and a cow," Tenāli said, "bring all of them into the house to live with you."

'That would be a silly thing to do,' thought Vasu. But he did it anyway. His house was already small, and with all those noisy animals in it, there was no

"Making ideas work"

room at all. He returned to Tenāli Raman and cried, "I need more space, more room and peace! The animals have crowded my house and are so noisy that I can't think at all!"

"Don't panic! Now take all those animals out of your house and put them back in the barn (shed)," Tenāli replied.

When Vasu Rao had put all the animals comfortably back in the barn, he went into his house. To his utter astonishment, the house suddenly looked remarkably bigger! Without the animals inside, his house was now quiet too! And his problem was solved without spending anything.

Life's Lesson

"Every problem has a 'context'. If you change the 'context', the problem may cease to exist."

Wise Cracks

- ☼ The good and the bad are only opinions and it is in our power to think as we please.
- ☼ Events remain the same, only the perception and opinions change.
- ☼ We are more or less, slaves of our opinions.
- ☼ Our opinions depend upon our lives and habits.
- ☼ He who never changes his opinions and/or corrects his mistakes, will never be wiser.
- ☼ So, opinions should be judged and directed wisely, with open mind.

Quotable Nugget

"As our inclinations are, so our opinions would be."

Proverb

Code of
Brilliance

One day, Tenāli Raman visited his relatives, who were landlords and lived in Raichur Doab. Tenāli borrowed 1000 varahas (gold coins) from his relatives and headed towards Hampi. On his way, Tenāli encountered a robust Thug (cheat) who posed himself to be a self-contained sadhu. The Thug came to know of Tenāli's possessing plentiful varahas by looking at his plump pockets. He craftily managed to accompany Tenāli on his journey on the pretext of visiting his (Thug's) kin living in Hampi.

On the way, the Thug happened to win the confidence of Tenāli by his saintly attire and gospels. As night descended, both Tenāli and the Thug decided to spend the night at a highway inn. During the intervening night, the Thug decided

"Strategic partnership"

to rob Tenāli of his gold coins. With evil intentions, the thug followed Tenāli like a parasite, a bloodsucking leech. He engaged Tenāli in religious discourses and saintly tete-a-tete. As the cold night fell, both spread their blankets. Tenāli soon fell asleep. The Thug got up stealthily and searched Tenāli's pockets, his bag, and even his bedclothes. But he couldn't find even a trace of gold coins. Disappointed, he too fell asleep, wondering where Tenāli could have hidden his gold coins. But when he woke up early next morning, Tenāli was up already, his pockets bulging with the money. Again, they talked of this and that, and resumed their journey.

It was evening again and on their way they found a boarding house to stay. As the chilly night unfolded, both of them spread their blankets and went to bed. Tenāli, as night before, was the first to fall asleep. The Thug kept awake and again silently searched Tenāli's belongings underneath his pillow, his bed and everywhere. But the money wasn't to be found anywhere. Disheartened and dejected, he too fell asleep, quite baffled.

Early next morning, Tenāli and the Thug resumed their journey. When they reached the city gates, the Thug stopped and asked Tenāli, "The journey was indeed a pleasing one but where did you keep your money the last two nights? I'm curious to understand this riddle which is troubling me for the last two days."

"Ahhhhh..." said Tenāli with a chuckle, "that's where the fine art of thuggery lies. I knew your evil intentions, so every night I hid the money right underneath your pillow. You never looked for it there. How would you find it by looking into my clothes, my pillow, and my bed?"

Hearing this, the stunned Thug saluted Tenāli and said, "No wonder you're the Master Thug," and left with a clumsy face.

Life's Lesson

Most people have 'standard thinking systems' and use 'tunnel vision'. They cannot think 'outside the box, they become 'sustainers.' The others who use 'innovation' and 'break the mould' are invariably, the 'WINNERS'.

Wise Cracks

☼ Self-assessment of our skills, thoughts and conduct is essential.

☼ We possess skills, but lack introspection. We remain so occupied to our shallow pursuits in the rat race of greed and ambitions that we lose balance and fail to read the situations correctly.

☼ Practised wisdom is required to save life and property.

Quotable Nugget

"Look around the habitable world! How few know their own; or knowing it pursue."

William Drummond

Spectacular Water

Once a distraught lady living in Tenāli Raman's neighbourhood came to him and complained that she was forced to quarrel frequently with her annoying mother-in-law. Such bickering was causing enough commotion in their house and thus, she requested an easy solution from Tenāli.

Tenāli Raman patiently listened to the lady's problem and gave her a bottle of water saying, "It is the water from a holy land. Whenever your mother-in-law makes an irritating comment which annoys you, just fill your mouth with this holy water and keep it in your mouth for just two minutes. Be careful not to spill it or swallow it till the end of two minutes. Then you can drink it and continue the conversation. Your problem will be solved."

"A sacred affair"

Thanking Tenali, the lady went home with the bottle of holy water.

Next week, the lady returned to Tenāli and gladly reported that the water was working wonderfully. She requested another bottle of water from Tenāli. Tenāli acceded to her request and gave another bottle to the lady. This exercise continued for a month successfully.

After a month, when the lady again came to Tenāli Raman seeking another such bottle of water, he told her, "Now you need not come to me for the water. You can refill it at home from your own well." This astonished the lady.

Later, the lady learned how the trick of Tenāli worked. The water just prevented her from quickly reacting to her old mother-in-law's comments impulsively and thus, restricted the outburst of her anger. Thereafter, she practised this principle of patience to control her anger and led a peaceful life thanking the witty Tenāli.

Life's Lesson

"Alexandre Dumas, once said that there is nothing more galling to angry people than the coolness of those on whom they wish to vent their spleen. Being calm is the only remedy.

Wise Cracks

- ☼ Anger is momentary insanity and is just one letter short of danger.
- ☼ The greatest and easiest remedy available for controlling anger is delay.
- ☼ He who can suppress a moment's anger can prevent a day of sorrow.
- ☼ If we keep our cool, we can command everybody.

Quotable Nugget

"Let not Sun go down, upon you anger."

St. James

A Bonafide
Verdict

*O*nce four friends started a business of cotton. They owned a godown in Hampi for storage of cotton bales. Finding that cotton saplings attracted large number of rats to the godown, a brisk and invigorating cat was introduced by them collectively to check the rodent menace.

All four friends loved the cat so much that they assigned to themselves one foot each of the cat for decorating it with pair of gold jingles. As a result, each foot of the cat was bejewelled with gold jingles and regularly looked after by the respective caretaker of the cat's foot so assigned.

Soon, the cat outdid its job and marvelled in keeping the rats at bay. Once, while performing its duties, the cat jumped from the top of a pile of bales. As a

"Simply a misfit"

result it started limping on one foot. So, the friends applied some balm and tied a long strip of muslin cloth as bandage around the wounded foot. Soon, the bandage got loose and the cat unaware of the long narrow cloth that was trailing behind her, sat near the fireplace, and when the cloth began to burn, she ran helter-skelter and fled into the godown itself, where the entire stock of cotton was reduced to ashes in a moment.

As all four friends had assigned one foot each of the cat to themselves, the injured foot belonged to one of them. So, the other three friends charged him with the damages, which they claimed from him desperately. The troubled friend asserted his innocence and defended himself by stating that the entire episode was just an accident for which no one should be held responsible, but the other three insisted to claim the damages from him.

The matter went to the Royal Court for settlement and hearing the arguments from both the sides, King Krishnadeva Rāya entrusted Tenāli Raman to decide the case thoughtfully and thereby maintain the sanctity of the imperial Court.

Tenāli thoroughly analysed the event that had happened and announced, "The injured feet had no responsibility, for it was taken into the godown with the trail of fire by the other three healthy feet. So, the damages have to be paid by the owners of the healthy feet to the owner of the limping foot!"

On listening to the judgment, the three friends were taken aback and realised their fault of acting cunningly. The King appreciated the reasoned decision of Tenāli and reprimanded the three for their misconduct.

Life's Lesson

"It is said, 'There is no right, there is no wrong. But thinking makes it so'. And it is the same reference in Frederick Langbridge quote. Two men look out through the same bars, one sees the mud, and one the stars. The wise man looks at a problem from multiple perspectives."

Wise Cracks

- ☼ Events remain the same everywhere; the 'point of view' is the only difference.
- ☼ What some of us consider failure, others think it to be success.
- ☼ Judge the events with logic and prudence.
- ☼ When looking at things be detached.

Quotable Nugget

"Two men look out through the same bars;
One sees the mud, and one the stars."

Frederick Langbridge

A Perfect Lesson

Once there lived a dishonest money-lender namely, Koteswara Rao in Hampi. Koteswara used to lend money to the deprived villagers but charged exhorbitant interest from them. As a result, Koteswara Rao earned a lot more than he gave.

This unfair conduct of Koteswara Rao was brought to the notice of Tenāli Raman by the poor villagers. Tenāli Raman taking note of the agony of the villagers, at once devised a plan in his mind to teach Koteswara a bitter lesson.

The next day Tenāli Raman went to Koteswara Rao and said, "Sir, I have arranged a large feast at my house and I am in an urgent requirement of two large vessels for cooking. I request you to kindly rent me two large vessels for one day."

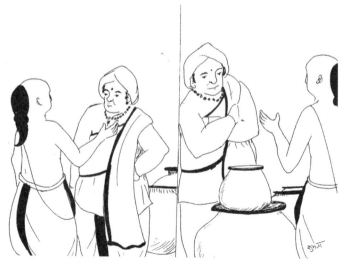

"Tilting at the windmills"

"Ofcourse, you can take them," Koteswara Rao said eagerly, "but you have to pay me five varahas as rent."

Tenāli Raman agreed to Koteswara's demand and gave him five varahas in advance and took the vessels home.

The following day, Tenāli went to Koteswara with four vessels, two big and two small. On his way, Tenāli had purchased two small vessels of the same shape as that of the large ones. On reaching Koteswara's house, Tenāli explained, "Sir, here are your two large vessels. Your two vessels were pregnant at the time of my borrowing them from you. They gave birth to these two small vessels early this morning, so all these four vessels belong to you."

The miserly Koteswara Rao was overjoyed to get two extra vessels. He took all the four vessels from Tenāli without speaking a word and kept them in his house.

A few days later, Tenāli again approached Koteswara Rao. He said, "Sir, I am holding a grand feast for the Brahmins of the city at my place tomorrow, so I need some large vessels for cooking. I will return them after two days to you."

The money lender was cheerful to hear Tenāli's requirement and immediately arranged a cart and loaded it with large vessels.

While giving the vessels to Tenāli, Koteswara said, "I am giving a cart loaded with large vessels to you. My vessels are pregnant. You must take due care of them and the baby vessels they beget."

Tenāli assured Koteswara Rao that he will do so and left his place.

Weeks passed by but Tenāli did not return with the vessels. Koteswara Rao was annoyed. He himself hurried to Tenāli Raman's house and said irritably, "You had promised to return the vessels within two days but it has been a long time now. I want them back immediately. Give all my vessels to me."

"But, Sir, this is not possible. Unfortunately your vessels died at the time of child birth," said Tenāli sadly.

"Oh! You are a cheat! You are a trickster! How can my vessels die!" roared Koteswara.

Tenāli Raman explained, "Sir, I am not telling lies. As you know that some expectant ladies give birth to their babies safely, while others die giving birth to the child. In the same way, your vessels have died at the time of childbirth. I took all the care to keep your vessels hale and hearty. But they died during childbirth."

Koteswara shouted, "How can the vessels die? How can the vessels have babies? You are a cheat. I'll take you to the Royal Court for deceiving me."

Their argument grew stronger and ultimately they went to the King. In the Royal Court, King Krishnadeva Rāya heard the arguments of both the parties. Then he asked Koteswara Rao, "Why did you accepted the baby vessels the first time, didn't you know that vessels don't beget babies?"

Koteswara Rao stood silent bowing his head. "If you believed Tenāli Raman earlier, then you must accept that they are dead now," the King said.

Now Koteswara Rao had nothing to say but to accept the decision of the King. Thus, Tenāli Raman very cleverly taught a lesson to the miserly Koteswara Rao.

Life's Lesson

"Greed often spurs dishonesty. And dishonesty is like a boomerang. Just when you think all is well, it hits you on the back of the head."

Wise Cracks

- ☼ Integrity and honesty are the steps to true happiness.
- ☼ Honesty is the best policy to adopt.
- ☼ Immoral acts bring disgrace.
- ☼ Immorality is a vice, sin and crime.

Quotable Nugget

"Dishonesty is like a boomerang. Just when you think all is well, it hits you on the back of the head."

H. Jackson Brown

A Calculated Act

$\mathcal{D}$ivakarla Prakasam, a trader from Kampili lost his way while crossing the dense woodlands along the countryside. As he tried to reach the nearest city of Hampi, he accidentally rode off the road into a deep ditch overturning his cart. Though he escaped miraculously, the cart was struck deep in the mud and his horse died while trying to pull the cart out.

Divakarla dismally walked to the nearby cluster of houses to seek help. Seeing Tenāli Raman standing outside his house, Divakarla approached him and explained the entire tragic event. He sought his help. "Shankara can get you out of that ditch," said Tenāli self-confidently, pointing to an old horse standing in the backyard of his house. Divakarla startlingly looked at the frail horse and at Tenāli who just stood there repeating, "Yes, old Shankara can do the job." Divakarla figured that he had nothing to lose at that odd moment.

"Came, shocked and conquered"

The two men and old Shankara made their way to the ditch. Tenāli hooked Shankara to the heavy cart with a thick rope. With a snap of the reins, Tenāli shouted, "Pull Rajulu! Pull Soma! Pull Ramaiah! Pull Venu! Pull Mani! Pull Vijaya! Pull Shankara!"

It was a wonder. The old thin horse Shankara pulled the heavy cart out of the ditch.

Divakarla was shocked to see all this. He thanked Tenāli Raman, patted Shankara, and eagerly asked, "Why did you call out all those names before you called Shankara?"

Tenāli grinned and said, "Old Shankara is just about blind. As long as he believes that he's part of a team, he doesn't mind pulling."

Divakarla was more astonished to listen to Tenāli's reply than the act he witnessed earlier, the old horse pulling out a heavy cart.

Life's Lesson

"Teamwork is the new mantra. 'The boat won't go if we all don't row' — Harvey Wackay. And often, your individual strength greatly increases, when you know you are part of a 'team'."

Wise Cracks I

- ☼ Individual alone cannot solve the bigger problems.
- ☼ Problems become easier when a team solves.
- ☼ Teamwork is highly motivating and encouraging
- ☼ When spider's webs unite, they can tie up a lion.
- ☼ Union has strength.
- ☼ It is faith that does miraculous deeds.

Wise Cracks II

- ☼ The limit of man's achievement is his 'will'.
- ☼ He who is firm will mould the world to himself.

Quotable Nugget

"People do not lack strength; they lack will."

Victor Hugo

The Slippery Travellers

*A*n old woman ran a small flower shop in front of the Virupaksha temple in Hampi to earn her meagre livelihood. Once, four travellers visited the temple to pay obeisance and purchased some flowers from the old woman. During the purchase of flowers, the travellers asked the woman to keep in her custody their little bundle and in the meantime, they will visit the temple. They told her to give it back only when all the four were present.

Later, one of them returned alone and tricked the old woman into giving him the bundle. Soon the other three also came to collect the bundle from the

"spoilt brats"

woman. The poor woman explained them of her having already given the bundle to the man who had come earlier alone.

The three travellers were very angry and went astray. They took the old woman to the Bhuvana Vijayam for deciding the case. King Krishnadeva Rāya listened to their complaint and requested Tenāli Raman to decide the case amicably.

"So, you see, Sir, she has to pay us the compensation now!" the three cried.

"But why would she compensate you? She will give you the bundle itself," said Raman, and pausing a little, he added, "provided all four of you are present here to receive the bundle. She won't give the bundle to the three of you. Bring the fourth one. Come together and collect the bundle."

There was a sudden laughter in the Court and the three nasty men realised that they had lost the case.

Life's Lesson

"An X-ray penetrates through the flesh to reveal the bone. A rational and wise mind, can pierce through the 'mask' of chicanery and deceit to reveal the true 'face'."

Wise Cracks

☼ You can easily deceive some of the people all the time, and all of the people some of the time, but you can't deceive all of the people all the time.

Quotable Nuggets

"Everyone is born sincere and die deceivers."

Marquis De Vauvenargues

Guessing Game

Once while Bhuvana Vijayam was in progress, a serious discussion ensued amongst the ashtadiggajas and the courtiers to ascertain as to 'who is the most significant person responsible for the overall prosperity of the kingdom?'

Ramaraja Bhushana, one of the ashtadiggajas said confidently, "Undoubtedly, the prosperity and achievement of any kingdom depends on the King of that State. The emperor besides efficient administration of the empire also protects the civil and personal rights of his subjects and thereby brings affluence in his state. The King safeguards the freedom of the State from internal rebellions and external onslaughts. He also maintains the law and order machinery."

"Ramaraja! I too agree that the monarch certainly is imperative for the

Voice of dissent

prosperity of the state, but he alone is insignificant. What is the assurance that the King will not be immoral and cruel? If a King happens to be wicked, the downfall of the kingdom is certain," said King Krishnadeva Rāya.

Queen Mohanangi interfered and said assertively, "I hold that people are the real asset of any Empire. The inhabitants are accountable for the fortune of that state. I opine that common citizens like peasants, artisans, labourers, potters, blacksmiths, goldsmiths, carpenters, barbers, weavers, painters, etc. are the backbone and moral fibre of the state. Only these people with their devotion and efforts add multifold richness not only to themselves but to the state too."

King Rāya disagreed and said, "How can it be possible that the people alone bring prosperity to the state. They being illiterate have to depend on the King, the ministers and the brahmins."

The Mahapradhana (Prime Minister) said, "The Pradhana (Minister) is the most important person for the flourishing of a state."

To this the King replied, "How can it be? The Mahapradhana and Pradhana also have to depend on the King; nevertheless an able minister may also take repulsive steps which might result in complete damage to the state."

"I think the Dandanayaka (Commander) is the most important person for the prosperity of the state," said the Dandanayaka.

"Then there will always be war and unrest, with no peace in the state, in absence of the King's control over them," interjected the King.

Allasani Peddana, another ashtadiggaja suggested, "The most vital element is the condition of the forts in the state."

The King immediately disagreed, "Absolutely not. The troops are much more important than all the forts."

"The Brahmin is the most significant body," said Thathacharya, the Rajaguru.

"What is your opinion about it, Tenāli Raman?" disagreeing to everybody's contentions, the King asked Tenāli Raman who sat in a corner soundless.

"Your Majesty, I disagree with the Rajaguru's statement. Whether a person is good or bad, it has no relation to being a brahmin. A good person, irrespective of being a brahmin or not, would always be beneficial to the state, whereas even a Brahmin can cause enormous loss to the state," said Tenāli Raman politely.

The Rajaguru angrily reacted to this, "Tenāli you are blaming the priestly brahmins. I am sure no Brahmin can ever cause any harm to his king or the state. The brahmins are sincere and devoted always to the King and the Kingdom."

"Rajguruji, I shall prove your claim wrong. An evil person who may even be a brahmin, can stoop low to any extent for the sake of money," Tenāli Raman replied.

Seeing that the arguments were getting heated, the King adjourned the meeting.

Months passed by and everyone forgot the whole debate. Tenāli Raman apprised the king of his scheme to disapprove the comments of Rajaguru and went to ten prominent brahmins of the city. He told them that king Rāya desires to distribute gold sovereigns in silver plates to ten chosen brahmins of Hampi.

The brahmins were overjoyed and expressed gratefulness to Tenāli Raman for such distinction. They said, "We will just come after taking our bath."

"There is no time left for bathing. The emperor is eagerly waiting lest the auspicious time for donation may lapse, forget your bathing," stressed Raman.

"In that case I shall call other brahmins," asserted one of the brahmins and he rushed to call other brahmins.

"Wait please, Tenāli, allow us to just sprinkle some water on our hair. This will be treated as equivalent to a bath as per religious doctrines," added one of those brahmins.

Tenāli Raman did not reply and kept waiting quietly. The Brahmins sprinkled water on their individual heads, applied the religious mark and vermilion on their foreheads, and reached the Bhuvana Vijayam cheerfully following Tenāli. On seeing gold sovereigns in big silver plates kept in the Royal Court by the king, they got breathless with bliss.

When the King was about to donate the sovereigns to the chosen brahmins, Tenāli interrupted, "My Lord, I think you don't mind making the donations even if these Brahmins had no bath. These poor fellows were in a great hurry to reach and receive donations here, and hence just sprinkled water on their heads."

The King got infuriated and asked, "Is it true?" The brahmins were confused. They accepted slowly that they had no bath and slipped off from the Court quietly.

Tenāli Raman impressed upon the Rajaguru, "Rajaguruji, what do you have to say now on the debate held that day? Tempted by money and gifts, the priestly brahmins even forgot all those religious rites and rituals. One does not get a higher pedestal just by being a brahmin. This proves the Queen's argument that common and devoted citizens are more important than the priestly brahmins. Under the able guidance of a King and his wise Pradhanas and Adhikaris, the common people can bring prosperity to the state in no time."

The Rajaguru had nothing to say but nod in agreement.

Life's Lesson

"No man is an island, sufficient into himself. For success of countries or corporators you need leaders and followers. You need achievers and sustainers. You need a balance of thinkers and doers. Everyone contributes. To talk about who contributes none, is idle talk.

Wise Cracks

- ☼ People are the power of a country.
- ☼ The success or business of a country depends on its people.
- ☼ A management concept is meaningless without a shrewd understanding of people.

Quotable Nuggets

"If you want 10 days of happiness, grow grain. If you want 10 years of happiness, grow a tree. If you want 100 years of happiness, grow people."

Harvey Mackay.

"What makes a nation strong is not brigades, but its citizens' virtues."

Anonymous

Nine of Ten

Once, King Sri Krishnadeva Rāya and Tenāli Raman happened to cross the vast scorching Thar Desert mounting on camels. The holder of the camels was urging his herd of ten camels forward to the destination. King Rāya and Tenāli were mounted on separate camels and the rest of eight camels were carrying the King's articles. The King's small royal entourage followed them on their horses.

After covering a few miles across the blazing desert, the fatigued camel Holder mounted one of his camels. Riding the camel, the holder counted his camels in the herd. Finding the camels only nine in number, the holder immediately dismounted the camel and walked back in search of the lost one. Seeing no

"Feeling left out"

sign of any camel, he thought that he had lost his camel in the wilderness of the desert. He discontinued the search and hurried towards his camels, grieved and dismayed. There he counted the camels and to his great joy, he found all the ten of them. Happily, he again mounted one, and after a while he thought of counting his camels once more.

Again, the holder found his camels to be only nine instead of ten! He got down puzzled, and started the dismal search again. The lost camel could not be found. He rushed back to the herd, and counted it, he was surprised to see that all his ten camels were lazily walking along. He blamed the blazing heat of the desert for the peculiar situation and got mounted on the last camel, counting the rest for the third time. To his amazement, he again found the camels to be only nine. He just couldn't understand why one camel was missing from the herd. He jumped down and tiredly repeated the counting process. There again he found ten camels! This continued for several times.

King Rāya and Tenāli were pitifully observing all this and were baffled to see the dilemma which the holder was facing. Both felt distraught at the weird behaviour of the holder whose act was making the tiresome and dull journey more irksome in the baking barren desert.

At last, the holder discovering a camel less in the herd and unable to tolerate the loss of his dear camel sought the advice of King Rāya and Tenāli for his catch-22 situation.

"Sir, I started my journey with a herd of ten camels. But now I could find only nine. Where has one camel gone?" asked the disgruntled holder. When enquired he narrated the whole incident of counting and recounting. Pacifying the holder, Tenāli advised, "My dear friend, the desert Satan is really crooked. The Satan might be taking toll over your camels to quench its thirst. An easy solution to your problem is that you should walk and have all your ten camels in place rather than ride a camel and lose one."

"I think you are absolutely right. I should walk rather than mount a camel", the holder grumbled.

Resuming their journey, King Rāya and Tenāli smiled at each other for rescuing the poor holder of his trouble.

Life's Lesson

"Ignorance is bliss, when it is policy to be wise. In time, we can use the laser beam of learning to dispel the fog of ignorance."

Wise Cracks

- ☼ There is nothing more frightening than ignorance. Ignorance ruins the pleasure.
- ☼ Ignorance is the worst fault.
- ☼ Ignorance needs to be removed by knowledge.

Quotable Nugget

"To be ignorant of one's ignorance is the malady of the ignorant."

A. B. Alcott.

Blinded
by Lure

𝒯rade and commerce flourished in the Vijayanagara Empire under King Krishnadeva Rāya. Business was widely carried on with countries like China, Sri Lanka, Portugal and Central Asia.

Once the Emperor of China sent some juicy peaches for King Rāya as a token of gratitude. Along with the peaches was a note of the Chinese Emperor stating that the fruit was bestowed with the unique quality of imparting long life and vitality to anyone who ate them.

As the bucket of fruits was being presented before King Rāya; Tenāli Raman could not control his temptation and uneasiness at the sight of ripened peaches.

"Visual delight"

Without seeking the permission of the King, Tenāli dared to pick up one of the luscious peaches and quickly bite into it.

At this, the King felt offended and was enraged. "You've bitten into a fruit meant for me!" he roared, "this . . . this is an utter insult of mine. For this you must die Tenāli!"

As Tenāli Raman was being taken away by the royal guards for the punishment, he grumbled severely and shouted, "What a dishonest man the Emperor of China is? He says the fruit will give longevity to anybody who eats them. I took just one bite and I'm about to die. O. . . . , what a fate awaits the one who eats an entire fruit!"

On hearing this, the King was greatly amused by Raman's wit. The King not only pardoned him but also gave him a dozen peaches for which Tenāli had risked his life.

LIFE'S LESSON

"Do not rush where angels fear to tread. To react spontaneously and unthinking displays an impetuous temperament. Wait, think, act – a good motto for anyone in life."

Wise Cracks

- ☼ Temptation or lure is the irresistible force which can land us in trouble.
- ☼ It is better to shun the bait, than to repent and struggle in the trap.
- ☼ It requires strength and courage to abandon temptation.
- ☼ It is better to get rid of temptation.

Quotable Nuggets

"Tempt not a desperate man."

William Shakespeare

"Take away the motive and you take away the sin."

Don Quixote

A Dauntless Act

Once while returning from Kembavi during a chilly winter night, Tenāli Raman happened to come across a group of soldiers gossiping around a campfire.

Tenāli Raman comfortably seated himself amidst the soldiers in front of the fire for protection from the rude weather. A few moments later, Tenāli Raman discovered all the soldiers to be connoisseurs and experts of warfare. Very soon, the soldiers engaged themselves in vivid discussions about their bravery experiences as warriors in the battleground. Each started giving an account of his happenings.

"Courage personified"

One elderly warrior narrated an incident where he had single-handedly slaughtered ten rival soldiers during the battle at Simhachalam. Listening to this occurrence, another hefty soldier sitting by his side gave an extensive account of the manner in which he held an entire enemy regiment at bay during the capturing of the Fort of Vinukonda. Still another described how he managed to flee from the jail confinements of the enemy during the ongoing war at Potnur.

Event after event, incident after incident laden with grit and valour, the recounting continued till late night. Everybody enjoyed the exciting episodes.

When they all had finished their narratives and had nothing more to boast, they looked mockingly at Tenāli Raman. "I don't think you have any such adventures or escapades worth telling," said one of the middle-aged fighters.

"Ahhhhh, but I have one," said Tenāli Raman.

"You have it!" said the bewildered soldiers sarcastically.

"Yes," said Tenāli Raman and continued to recite the incident, "Once while travelling from Bellamakonda, I chanced upon a large outsized tent. I cautiously entered the tent. There to my utter amazement, I found the largest man I had ever seen lying on a mat. I recognised him at once to be a dreaded dacoit who had been terrorising and horrifying that part of the country for decades by conducting massive plunders and mass killings!"

"What did you do then?" asked the soldiers, their interest now fully aroused.

"I took out my sword and cut off his toe and ran for dear life," said Tenāli.

"Only his toe!" said a puzzled soldier. "Why only a toe? You should have chopped off his head with your sword while you had the chance!" yelled another soldier breathlessly.

"Somebody had already done that," said Raman smiling. "The head was lying near the body."

They wanted to laugh but did nothing.

Life's Lesson

"It takes a small man to downrise large men with big egos, with only a grain of wisdom and a sharp tongue."

Wise Cracks I

- ☼ He who boasts of his own knowledge or valour proclaims his ignorance.
- ☼ They, who boast most, generally fail most, for deeds are silent.
- ☼ He who prides himself upon honour and wealth hastens his own downfall.
- ☼ It should be remembered that where boasting ends, there dignity begins.

Quotable Nugget

"Don't brag; it isn't the whistle that pulls the train."

T. Harry Thompson

"When you start crowing, you stop growing."

Albert B. Lord

Wise Cracks II

- ☼ Courage is not only the absence of fear or blindly overlooking danger, but it is the seeing and conquering of every situation with wit and intelligence.
- ☼ Wit is the salt of conversation that wins goodwill.
- ☼ No mind is thoroughly well-organised that is deficient in a sense of wit.
- ☼ Wit is the rarest quality to be met with among people of education.
- ☼ Wit is the lubricating oil of every situation which prevents friction. Of all the qualities, wit should be upheld.

Quotable Nugget

"Wit is a zero added to our moral qualities; but which, standing alone, represents nothing."

C. Jordan

Grain Gain

One day while Tenāli Raman was passing through a marketplace, he noticed a large crowd outside a poultry shop. He enquired into the matter. He learnt that a poor peasant had accidentally dropped a heavy sack of oats on a chicken, crushing it to death.

The chicken was small, worth only about five varahas (gold coins), but the owner of the shop had caught the peasant by his throat and was demanding fifty varahas. His argument for claiming such a heavy amount was that the chicken would have grown into a fleshy bird in another two years, had it not died. Then it would have fetched him the amount he was asking for.

"Gone without a trace"

As the quarrel continued and tempers rose, somebody from the crowd noticed Tenāli - the scholar, and everybody made way for him.

"Judge our case, My Lord!" said the poultry shop-owner bowing courteously to Tenāli. "This man, through his utter negligence and carelessness has caused the death of a chicken that would have fetched me atleast fifty varahas in another two years!" continued to explain the shop-owner. Fear had made the poor peasant's speech disorderly. Nobody could understand what the poor peasant was saying.

"The price put on the chicken is fifty varahas," said Tenāli, to the peasant, "I advise you to pay the shop-owner fifty varahas immediately."

There was a gasp from the crowd. Everybody had expected Tenāli to rule in the peasant's favour. The owner of the chicken was overjoyed. "They said you were fair in your judgments, My Lord," he said, rubbing his hands in glee. "Now I can say there is no one fairer than you!"

"The law is always fair," smiled Tenāli, "tell me, how much grain a chicken eats in a year?"

"About half a sack," said the poultry shop-owner.

"So in two years the chicken that has died would have eaten atleast a whole sack of grain," said Tenāli, "Then please give this man the sack of grain that you've saved as the chicken would eat no more."

The chicken owner turned pale. A sack of grain would cost more than fifty varahas. Scared by the teases and jeers of the crowd, the shop owner realised his unwarranted demand and declared that he would not take any money from the peasant, and fled into the safety of his shop.

Life's Lesson

"The arrogance of the rich, treading over the bodies of the poor, is sheer wickedness. No wonder the Holy Book says that it is easier for a camel to pass through the eye of a needle, than for a cruel rich man to enter heaven."

Wise Cracks

- ☼ Wickedness is weakness.
- ☼ A wicked person acts without reasonable ground.
- ☼ Wickedness tends to grow up by degrees. It may prosper for a while and God may bear the wicked, but not forever.
- ☼ A wicked person is not the idea of God, so a person should be honest in his conduct as honesty is the best policy.

Quotable Nugget

"Keep 5 yards from a carriage, 10 yards from a horse, and 100 yards from an elephant; but the distance one should keep from a wicked man can't be measured."

Indian Proverb

Joy in
The City of Joy

$\mathcal{D}$omingo Paes, the Portuguese traveller was always fascinated by Vijayanagara's (City of Victory) prosperity and affluence. But what enthralled him most was the wit and intelligence of Bhuvana Vijayam.

Once during his visit to the Royal Court, he asked the King, "Which is the most precious thing in your Kingdom?"

All courtiers thought for a while and responded hesitantly.

"The splendid Royal Palace is the most valuable thing of our Kingdom," declared the learned Rajaguru Thathacharya.

"changing the norm"

The ashtadiggaja Nandi Thimmanna said, "The Tirupati temple, the Virupaksha temple, the Kodandarama temple and the Vittala temples are the most valued things of our Empire."

Another ashtadiggaja Allasani Peddana said, "I think, the royal treasury is the most prized of all things."

So did the other ashtadiggajas and courtiers such as Pingali Surana, Dhurjati etc. gave varying opinions but Tenāli Raman kept quiet. None of the replies of the courtiers or the ashtadiggajas satisfied Domingo Paes.

So, the King asked Tenāli Raman to answer the question of Domingo Paes.

Tenāli Raman turned towards Domingo and said, "Sir, I think the most precious thing in our Empire is 'freedom'. The people in our kingdom are nobody's slaves. They are always free to live a joyful and contended life."

"Well, Tenāli Raman, I know you are a scholar. I request you to prove your opinion," said Domingo courteously.

Tenāli agreed to the suggestion and requested a few days time to prove himself.

The King said, "Sir, while Tenāli shall prove his opinion, you will be our royal guest and Tenāli will himself take care of all the arrangements to make your stay comfortable in the royal guesthouse."

Domingo was greeted in the royal guesthouse. Delicious dishes and all types of cuisines were made available to Domingo. He was provided with all royal luxuries during his stay. Maids and attendants were specially deputed to serve him. In short, all facilities were made available to Domingo during his stay in the royal guesthouse.

During the first two days, Domingo enjoyed the luxurious stay a lot. On the third day, he desired to go out for a stroll. When he reached the guesthouse gates, he was stopped by Kavalus (royal guards) and was not allowed to go outside. On asking, Domingo was made to understand that the guards had strict orders not to let Domingo go outside the guesthouse.

Domingo thought that the prohibition might be owing to security reasons. Still after three days, Domingo felt bored and aloof and desired to go outside for a leisurely walk. However, he was again stopped at the gates. This annoyed Domingo. This went on for a fortnight.

Domingo was provided all luxuries but was not allowed to go outside the guesthouse. He felt imprisoned. Now he was not happy in the guesthouse.

After three weeks, the King called for Domingo and asked for his well-being. Domingo complained, "Your Honour, it's miserable. I have not eaten for the last three days."

"But, didn't Tenāli made appropriate arrangements for you?" enquired the King.

"The arrangements were luxurious but I was not allowed to move outside the guesthouse. I was imprisoned to stay in the guesthouse for the last three weeks."

On inquiring from the Adhikaris (imperial officers), the King came to know that Tenāli Raman had given strict orders not to allow Domingo to go outside the gates of the guesthouse.

This agitated the King who called for Tenāli Raman and questioned him for such a rude behaviour towards the royal guest.

Tenāli passionately said, "Your Honour, I was just doing what the guest has desired. The other day in the court he had asked to prove that the most precious thing of our Empire is 'freedom'. By not letting him go outside the guesthouse and keeping him confined to the guesthouse for a period of three weeks has proved the point."

Hearing Tenāli's reply the King and Domingo both smiled and were pleased with Tenāli Raman.

Life's Lesson

"'Freedom is my birthright and I shall have it', was the refrain of our freedom fighters. People like Mahatma Gandhi and Nelson Mandela have suffered for decades, so that their countrymen will be free. Freedom for body, mind and spirit - is indeed the cornerstone for everything else that one may want."

Wise Cracks

- ☼ Freedom or personal liberty is of paramount importance.
- ☼ We should endeavour to be free not only physically but also from all the mental constraints as well.
- ☼ It is important to be one's own person.

Quotable Nugget
"Better to die on one's feet than live on one's knees."

Dolores Ibarruri

Flight of The
Imagination

Once King Krishnadeva Rāya dreamt of an extraordinary palace whose walls were built of brightly coloured tiles which reflected abundant light. The palace appeared to have submerged in daylight. In short, the palace was a kind of fairylike fortress.

The King was awestruck by the dream palace. For weeks he discussed only the palace and its marvels. The King even declared a hefty reward for anyone who shall construct such a palace for him.

When the ashtadiggajas and courtiers heard about the King's dream palace and the reward proclamation, everyone was amazed because they knew that dreams can't be true and realised. But none dared to tell it to the King.

King Rāya held an assembly of reputed architects and planners of the Empire and deliberated with them the issue of the dream fortress. The King even desired the architects and planners to build the dream palace for him.

"Barely a tale, heart of the matter"

Skilful draftsmen and builders were deputed for preparation of the blueprint for the dream palace. He ordered to take steps to procure special construction material for the dream palace. This caused huge outflow of funds from the royal treasury.

None intervened in the King's silly project because of fear of wrath of the King.

At last, the courtiers approached Tenāli Raman to save the treasury. He assured to find a solution.

One day, when King Rāya was attending to the court matters in the Bhuvana Vijayam, an elderly man entered the court crying, "O King! I have been robbed of my entire earnings. Please help me."

The King astonishingly asked, "What has happened? Please tell me in detail."

"I am ruined, O Lord," the elderly man wept and said, "I am Trivikrama from nearby Kamalapuram village. I have been left penniless. The State has stolen my entire life's savings. I am left impoverished and am worried for my children and poor wife."

"You mean to say that some dishonest royal Adhikaris (imperial officers) have taken away your earnings or your property?" the King asked angrily.

"Yes, but the royal Adhikaris were not alone. They were accompanied by . ." Trivikrama paused.

"Don't panic. You narrate me the entire episode. You are under my absolute security," the King said.

"Your Honor! When I was sleeping last night, I had a dream in which you entered my house accompanied by your Adhikaris and guards. Then you got hold of the trunk which contained my entire life's earnings and took it away."

"You foolish fellow . . . do you mean to say that I took your trunk of wealth away in your dream? Do dreams ever come true, you senseless man?" the King roared.

"You are right. Dreams never come true. Be it my dream or your dream palace. It is sheer madness to believe in them," Trivikrama said adamantly.

The King was stunned to hear and so were the courtiers. As everyone wondered for the elderly man's grit, Trivikrama removed his disguise of white beard and hair and there stood the witty Tenāli Raman.

Before the King could say anything, Tenāli reminded, "Your Honour! Please remember that I am under your absolute security. You must pardon me for my act."

The King laughed and realised his foolish plan of building a dream palace. He readily abandoned the project.

LIFE'S LESSON

"The ability to distinguish between wild fantasy and practical reality requires a mature mind capable of reason and judgement."

Wise Cracks
- ☼ Dreams are the children of idle brain.
- ☼ All dreams can't be realised.
- ☼ A realistic view to sort and understand dreams is required.

Quotable Nuggets

"We sometimes congratulate ourselves at the moment of waking from a troubled dream: it may be so the moment after death."

Nathaniel Hawthorne.

"Dream is the wife, who must talk; sleep is husband who silently suffers."

R. N. Tagore

An
Eye Opener

$\mathcal{K}$ing Krishnadeva Rāya was fond of doing heavy exercises daily in the morning. He regularly applied oil on his body and thereafter worked out till all oil came out in the form of sweat. This was followed by a long ride on his horse.

Once the King started leading a sedentary lifestyle. He stopped all sort of exercises. The King overate and as a result, he grew fat and heavier. The King's temperament also underwent a sea change.

Noticing this, the royal physicians cautioned the King against the ill-effects of overeating and risks posed by obesity. They advised the King to abstain from overeating and to take due care of his health. The repeated advice of the physicians and doctors for asking him to eat less made the King so angry that

"Getting the facts right"

one day he announced a reward for anyone who could find him an easy and a proper cure.

But there was one condition: those who failed would have their heads off.

None dared to advice the King in this regard. The situation became precarious and as usual Tenāli Raman was approached by the courtiers for a remedy. Tenāli heard the problem and assured the courtiers of a viable solution.

The next day, an astrologer predicted that the King had only a month left to live. When the King came to know of this, he got furious and upset. The astrologer was ordered by the King to be imprisoned for a month, so that his prediction could be put to test.

So, the astrologer was promptly thrown into the prison. The King was so terrified of the prediction that he hardly ate anything and lost a lot of weight over the month.

When one month passed and nothing happened to King's life, he summoned the astrologer and roared, "Tell me, why I shouldn't behead you?"

The astrologer replied patiently, "My Lord, look in the mirror, and see yourself cured!"

King Rāya was astonished to find himself slim and healthy.

Then the 'astrologer' told King Rāya that he was in fact a physician and has done this on the advice of the court jester Tenāli Raman. By frightening the King to death, he had made the King eat less and that had cured him.

The King felt delighted by Tenāli's wit. He promised never to be a victim of bad habits.

Life's Lesson

"Bad habits are easy to acquire – difficult to give up. Sometimes it may be justified to use fear, rather than reason – to snap out of bad habits."

Wise Cracks

- ☼ Habit is a sort of second nature.
- ☼ The chains of habit are too weak to be felt till they are too strong to be broken.
- ☼ Bad habit is an easy victory of time over will and it dies hard.
- ☼ Good habits result only from resisting temptation.

Quotable Nugget
"Habit is a stick to use, not a crutch to lean on."

A. G. Gardiner

Master
Stroke

*T*irumala, Tenāli Raman's close friend owned an Inn by the name of 'Deccan Suryam (The Sun of South)' in the capital city of Hampi. Tirumala was unable to make both ends meet, even though he did his best to draw customers by making the Inn comfortable, the services pleasant and the prices reasonable. So in despair, he consulted his clever friend Tenāli Raman.

After listening to his tale of woe, Tenāli said, "It is very simple. You must change the name of your Inn."

"Impossible!" said Tirumala. "It has been the 'Deccan Suryam' for generations and is well-known all over the Empire."

"No," said Tenāli firmly. "You must now call it 'The Five Bells (Panch Vāni)' and have a row of six large bells hanging at the entrance of the Inn."

Changing tactics.......against the tide

"Six large bells? But this is absurd. What good would that do?" said the astonished Innkeeper.

"Give it a try and see," said Tenāli with a smile.

Well, Tirumala gave it a try. And this is what he saw.

Every traveller who passed by the Inn walked inside to point out the mistake, each one believing that no one else had noticed it yet. Once inside, the travellers were impressed by the cordiality of the service and stayed on to refresh themselves, thereby providing the Innkeeper with the fortune that he had been seeking in vain for so long.

LIFE'S LESSON

"Most people prefer to dispense criticism rather than praise. It is human nature. They choose to pick out the faults of others, rather than look at themselves. A smart businessman channels this inclination to achieve his own goals, and he need not do this dishonestly."

Wise Cracks

- ☼ Sheer egoism is deflating which gives rise to criticism.
- ☼ Desire to seem clever, to find faults, to be talked about, to be remembered after death etc., delights people and causes them to criticise.
- ☼ We should not be afraid to face the music (criticism); as it may get us to lead the band someday.
- ☼ We would rather be ruined by praise than saved with criticism.
- ☼ The more active and fruitful our lives, the more we will receive criticism.

Quotable Nugget

"Don't be afraid of criticism. Anyone who can fill out a laundry slip thinks of himself as a writer. Anyone who can't fill out a laundry slip thinks of himself as a critic."

George Seaton

"Instead of putting others in their place, put yourself in their place."

Anonymous

The
Grand Plan

One summer morning, Tenāli Raman's wife was expecting a visit of her distant relative namely, Ādinārāyana Rāo from their native village near Tanjore.

She gave two ripe mangoes to Tenāli and asked him to slice them properly and serve the fruit with sandal sherbet when Rao visits their house.

While slicing the luscious mangoes, Tenāli Raman gave in to the temptation of the succulent fruit and ate a slice secretly. It was so sweet that Tenāli could not resist eating another slice. Then the madness of greed seized Tenāli and he ate all the remaining slices hurriedly without realising that he has emptied the platter.

Suddenly, Tenāli saw his guest Ādinārāyana Rāo coming towards his house. Tenāli thought fast and an idea emerged. Tenāli grabbed an old rusty knife from

"part of the treat"

inside and rushing to his wife told her that he couldn't slice the mangoes properly as the knife was blunt.

"Give the knife to me, I'll sharpen it," said Tenāli's wife and taking the blunt knife to a stone in the garden began to rub the cutting edge of the knife against it.

Leaving her to the task, Tenāli ran out to greet Ādinārāyana Rāo who was coming towards his house.

"Be cautious! Take heed!" Tenāli said pensively when he reached to Ādinārāyana Rāo, "Don't dare to come to our house. My wife has gone mad. She's planning to cut both your ears," continued Tenāli.

"What are you telling me? Cut my ears!" shouted Rāo astonishingly, "But why? I don't believe you!" yelled Rao.

"There . . . . . she is sharpening the knife," said Tenāli pointing towards his wife who was sharpening the blunt knife in the garden.

Ādinārāyana Rāo was perplexed. He saw that his host did indeed had a knife in her hands and was sharpening it with what looked to him like an unabated anger. He did not wait to find out why his host wanted his ears. Rāo turned around and started walking away as fast as he could.

Just then, Tenāli rushed back to his wife in the garden where she was busy sharpening the knife with full strength and told her that Adinarayana Rao had been acting very idiotically and was running away with the mangoes.

"What . . . . !" said Tenāli's wife oddly, "The greedy fellow! How crazy is he? Has he taken both the mangoes?!" she enquired.

"Yes," said Tenāli.

Hearing Tenāli, his wife ran after Ādinārāyana Rāo carrying the knife in her hand shouting, "Give me one! Give me one at least!"

Ādinārāyana Rāo thought that the lady was asking for one of his ears and ran for his life.

Tenāli silently observing the whole incident smiled gleefully and felt contented of eating the tempting mangoes secretly and also smartly saving himself of the folly of eating them.

Life's Lesson

"Irrational decisions are taken in the spur of the moment, where passion takes an upper hand. Then such actions have to be defended by lies and deceptions. Thus, there follows a drying up of a sense of self worth."

Wise Cracks

- ☼ Passion (desire) can compel us to do any act and to go to any extent.
- ☼ The worst of slaves is he whom the passion rules.
- ☼ Passion is the drunkenness of mind which makes us feel but never makes us see clearly.
- ☼ Our passions like fire and water are good servants but bad masters.
- ☼ We should take care to chastise (discipline) our passions than let passions chastise us.
- ☼ It is not poverty that causes sorrow, but greedy desires.

Quotable Nugget

"Where passion rules, how weak does reason prove?"

John Dryden

The Knotty Knot

Once a serious discussion ensued between King Krishnadeva Rāya and Tenāli Raman in order to ascertain whether people generally accept any matter easily or not. While the King stressed that people cannot be fooled easily, Tenāli opined that people can be made to believe anything effortlessly.

King Rāya said, "You can't make anybody to do whatever you wish."

Tenāli said, "Your Majesty! I can get the most impracticable job done from anyone. To prove this, I can even dare to make a person strike you publicly with a shoe."

"Breaking the myth"

"What? I challenge you to demonstrate so," said the King.

"I accept your challenge, Sir! But you have to give me sometime for it," replied Tenāli.

The King agreed to allow time to Tenāli. However after a few days, this challenge got lost in time and the King forgot this incident.

After about a month, King Rāya decided to marry the gorgeous daughter of a Tribal Chief from Coorg (Kodagu) province. The Chief was ignorant about the royal customs and rituals of Vijayanagar.

At this, King Rāya said to the Chief, "I only need your daughter in the marriage. The rituals and ceremonies vary in each State and you don't have to worry about them."

Still the Chief wanted to observe all customs and ceremonies of a Royal marriage.

One day Tenāli secretly met the Chief to explain the marriage rituals. The Chief was delighted and promised to keep secret the source of his information.

Tenāli then suggested to the Chief, "There is an old custom in the family of King Rāya that on completion of all rituals and ceremonies of a royal wedlock, the bride removes her own footwear and publicly throws it on the bridegroom. After that, the bridegroom takes the bride to his house. I want that this ritual must also be performed along with other rituals as this helps to maintain the sacred knot between the couple. For this, I have especially brought a pair of velvet shoes for the bride from Portuguese of Goa. The Portuguese further apprised me about this custom of shoe-throwing being prevalent in Europe as well."

When the Chief listened to Tenāli, he astonishingly asked, "Will it be proper for a wife to throw a shoe on her husband in front of everybody?"

Tenāli replied, "Though this ritual is followed in Royal marriages of Vijayanagar, you can ignore it if you have any hesitation."

At this, the Chief immediately reacted, "No... No... Please give it to me. I do not wish to leave any stone unturned in my daughter's marriage and for their prosperity."

After a few days, the marriage took place and all the rituals and ceremonies were over. The King was very happy and busy making arrangements to take the bride home. All of sudden, the bride removed her velvet shoe and smilingly threw it at the King in front of everybody. This infuriated the King. Just as the King was to roar in anger, Tenāli standing nearby whispered in the King's ear, "My Lord! Don't get furious. Kindly forgive her, this is all my doing. The bride is innocent." Saying this, Tenāli reminded the King of his challenge to prove his assertion.

The King laughed, lifted the shoe and returned it to the bride. The helpless bride clarified apologising, "I had to do this to complete the rituals."

The amused King said, "You were right Tenāli, people would easily believe any utterance."

Life's Lesson

"Many people go by rumours and hearsay. It is the wise person who collects the facts, evaluates these facts, cross-checks for accuracy and then converts information into knowledge, which can be used discreetly and appropriately."

Wise Cracks

- ☼ To act on gossips and rumours is not wisdom.
- ☼ Rumours are the most deadly microbe.
- ☼ Don't believe a rumour and don't jump at conclusion.
- ☼ Possession of facts is knowledge; the use of them is wisdom and the choice of them, education.

Quotable Nugget

"Facts are to the mind what food is to the body."

Edmund Burke

The
Dessert Taster

*K*ing Krishnadeva Rāya paid special attention to trade. Extensive trade was carried with countries like China, Sri Lanka and Central Asia. Foreign merchants and travellers used to visit Vijayanagar regularly.

Once a rich merchant named Rasool came from Persia to meet King Rāya. He was treated admirably. Graceful arrangements were made for his boarding and lodging in the Royal guesthouse. Special care was taken for the merchant's hospitality.

During daytime, Rasool went around the countryside to have firsthand experience of lush green paddy fields, tall stout palm trees, grooves of succulent

"Exotic dessert flavour"

banana trees and sprawling fields with abundant growth of slender juicy sugarcane. Rasool cherished this sight as these were totally amiss from his home country.

That night after dinner, the King ordered the royal cook to serve all the sweet delicacies and desserts such as Mysore Pāk, Shree Khand, Puranpoli and Modaka (all are Indian sweet dishes) to Rasool in his room. The royal cook served to Rasool all the sweet dishes but to the King's surprise, Rasool did not eat any of the sweet dishes. The King was apprised that Rasool did not even touched a grain of the sweet dishes and desserts offered to him. Instead, he insisted on eating the roots of these sweet dishes."

"Roots of Mysore Pāk, Shree Khand, Puranpoli and Modaka!" the King exclaimed in surprise. He had never heard of the roots of these sweet dishes, still he wished to get them as he always wanted his guests' every wish to be fulfilled. Next morning in the Royal Court, the King asked the courtiers to find the roots of Mysore Pāk, Shree Khand, Puranpoli and Modaka. But everyone expressed their inability to find any such thing as the roots of the sweet dishes.The King ultimately sought the advice of Tenāli Raman who assured King Rāya to arrange for the roots of the sweet dishes and desserts. And giving all assurances, Tenāli asked for a bowl and a large sharp knife.

Everybody in the court was surprised at Tenāli's tall assurances as nothing of such sort existed. An hour later, Tenāli returned to the Royal Court. He was holding a bowl covered with a piece of muslin cloth. With great joy and excitement he said, "Your Majesty, here are the roots of Mysore Pāk, Shree Khand, Puranpoli and Modaka!"

Everyone glanced at each other with surprise. The King also got curious and desired to see roots of Mysore Pāk, Shree Khand, Puranpoli and Modaka. Before Tenāli showed the roots of sweet dishes, Rasool was also called to the Royal Court. When everybody was present in the court, Tenāli said to Rasool, "Sir, here is your wish fulfilled. I have brought the roots of Mysore Pāk, Shree Khand, Puranpoli and Modaka as you had wished for."

Rasool eagerly took the bowl. He took off the cloth and keenly tasted what was served in it. He cheerfully exclaimed, "These roots of Mysore Pāk, Shree Khand, Puranpoli and Modaka are so sweet and tasty. They are not found in Persia and I am deeply spellbound by their exceptional taste which makes the taste of Deccan sweet dishes and desserts a pleasant experience."

As the King and the courtiers watched with their mouth wide open, Rasool contently chewed the pieces of sugarcane which Tenāli had cut into small pieces. The King and the courtiers laughed heartily and praised Tenāli for his intelligence.

Life's Lesson

"Truly learned and wise men have 'insight'. They are able to break through the superficial and get to the root of the problem. Therefore, they have greater abilities to solve seemingly intractable problems through 'insight' and a new approach."

Wise Cracks

- Men are not to be judged by their looks, habits and appearances, but by the character and their work.
- The real character of a person or a thing is not visible from outside but lies deep within.
- Character is revealed only by close analysis of a person or a thing amidst trying circumstances.
- Character is the man's greatest need and greatest safeguard. For ascertaining the character, a prudent vision is essential.

Quotable Nugget

Character is what you are in the dark."

Dwight Moody

Measure For Measure

King Krishnadeva Rāya was known as Abhinava Bhoja as he was a great patron of art and literature.

Once the King came to know about a versatile artist called Achyuta Rao living in Ketavaram. He pleasingly invited him to the Imperial Court and asked the artist to draw the King's portrait.

Achyuta Rao painted a magnificent portrait of the King. The King was left spellbound on seeing himself as a lively, royal and elegant Emperor in the portrait.

Achyuta Rao not only drew the King's portrait, but also presented the King with images of prominent characters from the Puranas and Holy Scriptures, of

Not rightly chosen

gods and goddesses, of men and women, and so on. Soon the artist became well-known for his genius. He became close and dear to the King.

One day, overwhelmed with joy, the King called Achyuta Rao and asked him to name a reward he wanted. When Achyuta Rao did not reply, the King, in the spur of a generous impulse, rewarded him with the post of Chief Minister in the Royal Court.

Though Achyuta Rao was a good man and a brilliant artist, he had no experience whatsoever of administration or governing a State. Soon everything was thrown into chaos because of Achyuta Rao's hasty and impulsive decisions and bad management of state affairs. People were unhappy over Rao's administration, but they did not dare to complain to the King because the King was very fond of Rao.

When the state governance became unbearably out of order, the ashtadiggajas and the courtiers finally approached and sought Tenāli Raman's help in getting rid of the new and inept Chief Minister.

Tenāli assured them of soon finding an inoffensive way to make the King realise his folly and to remove the artist from the Chief Ministership.

After a fortnight, Tenāli Raman invited the King, the queens, the ashtadiggajas and a few courtiers to his house for lunch. Meanwhile, Tenāli had found a very fine goldsmith whom he put on the job of preparing a splendid feast for the King and the royal guests.

The King and others sat for lunch and at Tenāli's order, the goldsmith began serving them. The moment they put the first morsel of food in their mouths, the invitees began to pant and rasp asking for water again and again.

Soon after tasting the food, the King realised that the food was badly cooked and was unbearably spicy. He was furious. "Tenāli! Who has cooked this food? Do you want all of us to suffer and die eating this horrible food?" the King roared.

In his usual humble way Tenāli said, "I beg your Majesty's forgiveness."

Then he introduced the goldsmith to the King, "I have never come across such an excellent goldsmith whom I have put on the job of cooking lunch for today's feast."

The King started laughing loudly, "Have you lost all sense, Raman? A good goldsmith should be employed to work on gold and silver but not on food. How did you get this funny idea of getting food prepared from him?"

Tenāli replied to the King courteously, "My Lord! If an artist can become a Chief Minister of the mighty Viajayanagara Empire, can't a proficient goldsmith become a cook?"

The King at once understood that Tenāli Raman had got a goldsmith to cook the food to make him realise his error of making Achyuta Rao the Chief Minister.

The King was saved from the embarrassment of removing Achyuta Rao from the post as when Achyuta Rao came to know of the awkward incident at Raman's house, he immediately resigned from his post.

Later Achyuta Rao told Tenāli that he was happy to remain only an artist.

Life's Lesson

"An indirect and inoffensive way to drive home a lesson, especially to colleagues and superiors, is to draw parallels and to give smiles. But doing this appropriately, is an art. An art that Tenāli had mastered – and by which he showed that you cannot have a square peg in a round hole."

Wise Cracks

- A pint can never hold a quart; and if it holds a pint properly, it is doing all that can be best expected of it.
- One has no more the capacity or competence of doing a job other than the job he is best meant for.
- You cannot learn to spell words by just sitting on a dictionary.
- The prudence in life is to put only round pegs in round holes instead of round pegs in square holes.

Quotable Nugget

"The things most people want to know about and do are usually none of their business."

George Bernard Shaw

Pursuit For
Justice

On his birthday celebrations, King Krishnadeva Rāya received plentiful of gifts from his subjects and neighbouring kingdoms. The various offerings also included fine flower pitchers gifted by the Sultan of Mysore Kingdom.

King Rāya assigned the royal attendants with the task of handling all gifts meticulously well particularly those exceptional and fragile flower pitchers.

One morning, when one of the royal attendants namely Jagannadh was busy performing his usual duty of cleaning all royal articles, a mischievous kitten ran by his side. The sudden arrival of the kitten stunned Jagannadh and he dropped a pitcher, breaking it completely into pieces.

"At crossroads"

The news of broken pitcher enraged the King who ordered Jagannadh to be sent to the gallows. Jagannadh pleaded his innocence but in vain.

Tenāli Raman tried persuading the King that the punishment awarded to Jagannadh was a hasty decision and in fact a ruthless act. Tenāli justified that Jagannadh ought to be forgiven by the King for an insignificant mistake rather than imposing such an extreme punishment. The King, however, refused to pay any heed to Tenāli's request.

The King's hasty decision of awarding an intense punishment to Jagannadh for a trivial mistake disturbed Tenāli Raman a lot. Tenāli was so concerned with the situation that he decided to have a meeting with Jagannadh. Next morning, on meeting Jagannadh, Tenāli gave him an idea to escape the perilous situation.

That evening, when Jagannadh was being taken to be hanged, he was asked to name his last wish. As his last wish, Jagannadh requested to see the remaining flower pitchers . . . those items which had caused him to be hanged, for one last time. When the flower pitchers were brought to him being carried by royal attendants, Jagannadh deliberately broke the remaining flower pitchers.

This act of Jagannadh further infuriated the King. On being asked why he broke the remaining pitchers intentionally, Jagannadh explained to the angry King that he had done so to save the lives of other royal attendants. Their lives are also at stake.

This reply of Jagannadh astonished the King who realised his mistake of making abrupt and hasty decisions on insignificant issues. King Rāya not only forgave Jagannadh but also made an apology to him who later told the King that it was the wisdom of Tenāli Raman that had saved his life. The King felt grateful to Tenāli for preventing him from committing such a sinful crime.

Life's Lesson

"It is impossible to live a life without a blemish. Making mistakes is normal, provided mistakes contribute to learning and the same mistakes are not repeated. If punishment is due for mistakes committed, such punishment should be proportional to the intensity of the error."

Wise Cracks I

- Any man may make a mistake. You can't get through this world without making mistakes.
- The fellow who makes no mistakes does nothing and that is a mistake.
- It is within the nature of all human to make mistakes, that's why pencils have erasers.
- To make no mistakes is not in the power of man, but to forgive is within the power of all human beings. And forgiveness is the noblest revenge and an attribute of the strong.

Quotable Nuggets

"To err is human, to forgive is divine."

Alexander Pope

"To err is human, but when the eraser wears out ahead of the pencil, you're overdoing it."

Josh Jenkins.

Wise Cracks II

- Haste is the devil that administers all things badly.
- 'Good' and 'quickly' seldom meet.
- Hasty climbers have sudden falls.
- Decisions should be taken with precision and acumen.

Quotable Nugget

"He who pours water hastily into a bottle spills more than what goes in."

Spanish Proverb

The Final Solution

One day, King Sri Krishnadeva Rāya became offended with his jester Tenāli Raman. King Rāya ordered him to leave his Empire. Tenāli obeyed the King's order and started his journey to leave the territory of the vast Vijayanagara Empire.

After some days, King Rāya while riding a horse happened to pass through a dense forest. At that very moment, he spotted a person climbing the top of a huge tree. Observing carefully, the King noticed that the person climbing the tree was none other than the scholarly Tenāli Raman.

The King moved near the tree and in an arrogant voice said, "Tenāli! I told you to leave my Empire. But you are still here? You have breached my orders!"

To this Tenāli answered meekly, "Sir, I obeyed your orders and left the Vijayanagara Empire and travelled far and wide. But, wherever I went, all the people there whom I asked told me that 'this land is under the dominions and command of none other than that of Sri Krishnadeva Rāya – the brave son of Tuluva Narasanayaka

"Down to earth"

and the greatest statesmen of Deccan India'. Now, My Lord as you are omnipresent and widespread, the only thing left for me is to go to the other world – that is the Heaven. And as you can see I have already started my journey in that direction by climbing this huge tree to reach the other world. Sir, this is the only solution which I am left with."

Listening to this, King Rāya became very pleased and contented with Tenāli's loyalty and integrity. He pardoned Tenāli Raman and immediately ordered him to return and embellish the Bhuvana Vijayam as one of his ashtadiggajas.

Life's Lesson

"Flattery is the food for fools, yet if such flattery has a large dose of truth, then it ceases to be flattery and metamorphoses into a 'compliment'. Such honest compliments begot friendship, loyalty and kindness. It is an art which is worth cultivating by seeing the positive qualities of everyone you meet."

Wise Cracks

- ☼ No one knows about your loyalty, integrity, talent. Turn them into action.
- ☼ Loyalty plays an important part in the life of a man.

Quotable Nugget

"An ounce of loyalty is worth a pound of cleverness."

Elbert Hubbard.

The Master's Move

One bitter evening, while returning from the Vithalaswamy temple after attending a royal ritual, Tenāli Raman got stuck in a wet and stormy night. Struggling with the ruthless weather, Tenāli anyhow succeeded in locating a nearby Inn. Completely drenched to the skin, Tenāli entered the Inn. He made his way to the fireplace to get its warmth but there were several other villagers warming themselves in front of the fire and he could not go near it.

As Tenāli stood helplessly shivering there, the Inn owner who knew him slightly, welcomed him and asked why he was looking so sad.

"While I was finding a safe place for myself to shield from this unruly weather, I have lost my bag containing twenty varahas (gold coins) which I received during the royal ceremony," said Tenāli uneasily.

"Better deal"

"Where did you lose it?" asked the Inn Owner, as the men who had been standing in front of the fire gathered around Tenāli and the Inn Owner to overhear the happening.

"Within a mile of this place, I'm sure," said Tenāli worried and hopeless. "I'll go in search of it first thing in the morning. Nobody is likely to travel by that barren road in this bad weather and the bag will certainly be there till morning."

"If I were you . . ." began the Inn Owner.

"Yes, yes, what would you have done . . . ?" interrupted Tenāli. "But first come, let us warm ourselves by the fire. See, everybody has sneaked out! Where do you think all of them could have gone in this foul weather?" Tenāli continued his talk avoiding his eyes as he has told a lie to send the people in search of the bag. He wanted a place near the fire.

"If I were you," said the Inn Owner, grinning, "I would have become a storywriter!"

Life's Lesson

"There are inexcusable real lies and there are seemingly harmless 'white lies'. Can white lies which harm no one else be condemned? These are the grey areas, in the world of ethical behaviour."

Wise Cracks

☼ Greed is the vice which makes us appear small and poor.

☼ Greediness needs to be overcome.

Quotable Nugget

"People who have little and want less are happier than those who have much and want more."

Anonymous.

Dog's Trail

One day Tenāli Raman went to a sweet shop to buy some sweets. Stray dogs used to gather outside the sweet shop as people visiting the sweet shop would usually throw some small pieces of sweets at the dogs from their purchases.

Tenāli Raman loved animals, so as he passed one of the stray dogs, he patted it gently on its head. The dog felt happy and wagged its tail passionately. Tenāli left it and entered the shop. The dog thought that Tenāli was intending to call it inside the shop, so it followed him in.

Just as Tenāli entered the shop, followed by the dog, the shopkeeper spotted them. The shopkeeper was just returning to the shop after buying some fresh sweets to sell. He rushed in after the dog and shouted at Tenāli, "Tenāli! How

"Execellence on field"

dare you bring your dog into my shop? Don't you know that it is dirty and full of fleas? Chase your filthy dog out of the shop at once!"

Tenāli was stunned to listen such offensive words of the shopkeeper. He turned to the shopkeeper and said, "Hey! What made you think that this is my dog? It is just a stray dog that followed me into the shop."

The shopkeeper was not convinced, he said, "Ohhh. . . .! Tenāli, you think you are very witty and clever, don't you? You can fool all the people in town, but you can't fool me. I know that it is your dog, because it followed you into the shop."

Tenāli giggled and said, "Sir! In that case this dog is your master!" The shopkeeper was shocked. He shouted, "What do you mean? How can this dog be my master?"

Tenāli smiled and said, "You followed the dog into the shop right? If you think that I am the dog's master because it followed me into the shop, then the dog is your master because you followed it into the shop!"

The shopkeeper realised his mistake. He could not find any argument with Tenāli's witty answer, so he said, "Ok! I'm sorry." Saying that he placed some sweets outside the shop and the dog ran out of the shop to eat them.

Life's Lesson

"Presumptions, assumptions and jumping to conclusions. It happens to all of us in many situations in life. It takes a mature mind to be able to reach the reality."

Wise Cracks

- ☼ Bad elements are like bad habits that follow us everywhere.
- ☼ Habit is either the best servant, or the worst of masters.
- ☼ Evil habits easily follow us wherever we go.
- ☼ Bad habits should be readily shaken off than mended.

Quotable Nugget

"Habits are, at first, cobwebs, then cables."

Spanish Proverb

Your Honour's
Honour Honoured

Once King Krishnadeva Rāya was so pleased with Tenāli Raman that he rewarded Tenāli profusely. The reward was so lavish that Tenāli found it quite difficult to carry all the gold coins (varahas).

Anyhow, with great difficulty, Tenāli managed to fill his pockets with the gold coins and tied a few handfuls of coins in his turban. The entire Bhuvana Vijayam was amusingly looking at Tenāli's act of pocketing the reward with utmost care.

Just when Tenāli turned around to respectfully bow to the King in gratitude, one of his well stocked and puffed pockets snapped open under the weight of the coins. With this, the coins spilled all around the floor and rolled off in all directions.

"His faithfully"

The entire court burst into laughter.

Noticing this, Tenāli recklessly moved around between the seated courtiers to gather the scattered coins from under the chairs, the carpets, the seats, the tables and from here and there and everywhere in a hurried manner.

Tenāli's gathering coins in such a hasty manner not only became a laughing stock for the courtiers but many of the envious courtiers felt contended at Tenāli becoming a fool publicly. Soon the entire court was filled with whispers and murmurs like 'What a greedy man Tenāli is?' 'Tenāli is really a shameless and greedy person. See how meanly he is gathering the coins? It's ridiculous to see an asthadiggaja doing such a measly act!'

All courtiers teased Tenāli of his strange act.

The King finding the act unbearable roared, "Tenāli! Please stop behaving foolishly. Stop searching the spilled coins. Such a measly act is uncalled for from a scholarly person of your stature."

"Your Honour! It is neither greed nor miserliness," said Tenāli dutifully. "I am worried about Your Honour and the divine respect. I need not tell you that the varahas (gold coins) I have spilled all around have your name and your face engraved on them. I don't want anyone stepping on the coins or them being kicked around or some broom sweeping them like dirt. So, I must collect each and every coin."

Listening to Tenāli's reply, the King smiled in admiration. Meanwhile, Tenāli continued his search for each and every coin peacefully and the courtiers watched the entire episode tightlipped.

Life's Lesson

"Life is an obstacle race where all of us are called to participate. Winners will be those who are able to convert the negatives into positives, those who can bring a new view to a problem and make others see it in a new light."

Wise Cracks

☼ The secret of a man's success exists in his insight into the moods of people, and his tact in dealing with them.

☼ Tact is an ability to make a person see lightning without feeling the bolt. Tact is most valuable for all those who have to climb and step out of the crowd.

☼ Without tact one can learn nothing. It is one of the first mental virtues, the absence of which is often fatal to the best of talents.

☼ Tact is a virtue that often makes us deal with odd situations graciously.

Quotable Nuggets

"One must change one's tactics every ten years if one wishes to maintain one's superiority."

Napoleon Bonaparte

"Tact is knowing how far to go is too far."

Jean Cocteau.

"Women and foxes, being weak, are distinguished by superior tact."

Ambrose Bierce.

Wicked Word

King Krishnadeva Rāya had great affinity for birds and animals. Once a bird-catcher came to the Royal Court and presented to the King a beautifully coloured bird in a cage. It was a strange looking bird which neither the King nor any of his courtiers had ever seen before.

The bird-catcher said to the King, "Your Honour, yesterday I was fortunate enough to catch this fine bird from the dense forests of Keladi for you. This bird is a matchless creature as it can sing melodiously and can also talk like a parakeet. It is multi-coloured like a peacock and can also dance like it. I have come here to sell this bird to you."

"Wild idea"

The King looking at the creature was enthralled to see a rare bird and agreed to purchase it from the bird-catcher. So much was the King impressed that he rewarded the bird-catcher with a hundred varahas (gold coins).

Tenāli Raman closely observing the bird and its catcher became suspicious of the conduct of the bird-catcher. He unexpectedly got up and said, "Your Honour, I don't think this bird can dance like a peacock in the rain. Indeed the bird is quite ugly and perhaps it has not taken bath for many days."

With these words, Tenāli picked a pitcher of water lying nearby and emptied it over the bird. The bird was completely drenched. All the courtiers looked surprisingly at the bird. The water flowing off the bird's body was coloured and soon the bird appeared in its original light grey colour.

The King looked at Tenāli in astonishment. Tenāli said, "Your Majesty! This is no rare, colourful bird. It is an ordinary pigeon of the woods."

"But Tenāli, how did you realise that this bird had been painted with false colours?" asked the King.

"Just from the bird-catcher's coloured nails, Your Honour! The colours he used to paint the bird are still present on his nails and fingers," explained Tenāli.

Hearing this, the bird catcher was arrested and put in prison. Tenāli was suitably rewarded by the King.

Life's Lesson

"This is what separates the men from boys. A deep curiosity, a keen interest, a perceptive mind. All these help to tear the mask and reveal the real face."

Wise Cracks

- ☼ Wickedness betrays the person himself who practises it.
- ☼ The act of dishonesty drinks one half of its own poison to make him happy.
- ☼ Though it is easier to betray than to remain loyal but dishonest motives can't be concealed forever. The pleasure derived from another's evil through cheating is momentary but it blackens the character forever.
- ☼ Honest ways should be exercised to earn a living and wealth.

Quotable Nugget

"Man's life is a warfare against the malice of men."

Baltesar Gracian

The
Blameworthy

$\mathcal{V}$ijayanagara became a thriving business centre under the rule of King Krishnadeva Rāya. Traders of many nationalities such as Arabs, Persians, Guzerates, Khorassanians settled in Calicut and did flourishing business.

Once a Persian merchant gave to King Rāya a plant bearing uniquely coloured and fragrant flowers which bloomed all round the year.

The King was spellbound by the unique plant and the flowers it bore. He ordered his gardener to get it planted right in front of his (the King's) bedroom, so that the flowers can be sighted from the window of his bedroom every morning and evening. The royal gardener did as the King ordered.

The King was delighted at the pleasing sight of the flowers.

"Deep impact"

One day, the gardener's goat slipped into the royal palace and ate the entire plant including its flowers. The gardener noticing the act of his goat was terrified to bring this act into the notice of the King.

Next morning, when the King glanced out of the window, he found the unique plant missing. He at once summoned the gardener and enquired about the plant. The gardener told the King that his goat ate the plant. The King got irritated and ordered death penalty to the gardener.

The news of the gardener's death penalty spread like wildfire. The gardener's wife pleaded the gardener's innocence but all in vain.

At last, the gardener's wife approached Tenāli Raman for relief. Tenāli hearing the entire episode and assured a solution to save the guiltless gardener. Tenāli advised the lady to do as directed by him.

Next day, people found the wife of the gardener beating her goat cruelly at the city's crossroads. The goat was tied to a hook and ruthlessly beaten with a stick.

The Adhikari (Imperial officer) and the royal guards learnt about this harsh act and reaching the spot got hold of the lady and took her straight to the King for her brutal act.

On being asked the reason for the lady's beating the innocent goat, the lady explained the King, "That goat is a devil. It is widowing me and making my kids orphans. It is responsible for bringing misfortune to me. It is responsible for the treatment which I am giving it."

"But it's a dumb animal. How can a goat widow you?" asked the King keenly.

"Your Honour, it is the same goat which ate your plant and flowers for which you have ordered death penalty to my innocent husband. Although this goat is the real culprit but it goes on bleating joyfully and munching on leaves leisurely. That's why I was beating the goat."

Hearing the lady's statement, the King pondered and announced, "Your husband won't die. I am pardoning the gardener. You can go without worrying and let the poor goat also bleat cheerfully and munch leisurely."

The King came to know of Tenāli's mind behind the entire episode and felt proud and satisfied.

LIFE'S LESSON

"You need to draw parallels to teach a lesson. Parallels are illustrative and practical – therefore, effective. If they are also simple – the effectiveness is even greater."

Wise Cracks

- ☼ Justice is the sum of all moral duty.
- ☼ The fundamentals of justice are that no one shall suffer wrong and public good be served.
- ☼ Injustice anywhere is a threat to justice everywhere.
- ☼ It is better that 100 guilty persons escape than to punish one innocent person.
- ☼ Fairness to all is what justice really is.

Quotable Nugget

"The love of justice in most men is simply the fear of suffering injustice."

Francois Rochefoucauld

Windfall Deal

$\mathcal{D}$uring the regime of King Krishnadeva Rāya, there lived a proud seth (moneylender). The seth bought an elegant house which was located right next to the house of a petty tanner. From morning till evening, the tanner converted hide into leather by treating it with tannin. From day one, the seth was put off by the persistent unpleasant smell emitted by the tannery.

Finding the foul smell unbearable, the haughty seth visited the tanner's house one day and threatened the poor tanner either to discontinue his occupation or vacate his house by selling it to him.

The poor tanner strongly refused to agree to any of the proposals made by the seth. At this, the seth became furious and further intensified his stir to get the

"Hidden truth"

tanner's house vacated by sending his vulgar attendants to the tanner's house daily and compel the tanner to vacate his house.

When the situation became disorderly and unbearable with the seth's attendants frisking the poor tanner every now and then, the tanner approached the Bhuvana Vijayam (Royal Court) and narrated the entire episode before the gentle King Rāya. Disgruntled at his peculiar situation, the tanner pleaded before the King,

"O King of Kings, the Vijayanagara kingdom has today flourished and acquired a significant place owing to your courage and patronage. But still, poor people like me are thwarted by rich and mighty who tend to snatch from us our livelihood. I seek your help, My Lord." Listening to the agony of the agrieved tanner, King Rāya requested Tenāli Raman to intervene and resolve the precarious situation cordially with his presence of mind.

Next day, Tenāli accompanied the tanner to his house and scanned the locality. Giving a brief thought, Tenāli suggested to the tanner, "Next time whenever the seth comes to you, simply accept his proposal of selling your house to him but on one condition . . . . that the possession of the house will be handed over to the seth only after a fortnight as the tanner has some pending chores to perform." The tanner was astonished to hear such a silly suggestion from Tenāli and remarked, "Sir, are you playing a prank with me? I will be ruined even if I think of selling this ancestral house to anyone. I have been carrying my trade from this place for the last four decades and all my clients are accustomed to this locality. A new place means complete loss of business and clientele."

"Do as I advise," recommended Tenāli. At last the tanner agreed to Tenāli's suggestion.

Next morning, the seth visited the tanner and put forth his same demand. The tanner patiently heard the seth and said, "Ok sethji, I am ready to vacate the house and sell it to you, but give me a fortnight or so to wind up some things." The seth consented and left the tanner's house in high stride.

A fortnight later, the overpowering smell coming from the tannery brought the seth to the tanner's doorstep again, "I understand your anguish, Sir," said the tanner when the seth told him that the smell had reduced his appetite largely. "But my mother is visiting me this week. I can't sell the house as long as she is around. Please wait for another week, until she goes away," continued the tanner as advised by Tenāli.

The seth agreed though with great reluctance. He waited for the tanner's guest to depart. In the beginning, the seth anxiously counted each day, impatiently waiting for one to finish and the other to begin. After a while, he found he was no longer all that interested in the week coming to an end. And when the week did end, the seth did not care to go to the tanner's house to ask him to leave. He had simply forgotten about it. He did not even care to ask the tanner to leave the house or utter a word in this regard when they met next, either.

The tanner was taken aback to find this abrupt change in the seth's attitude but felt quite relaxed. The tanner unable to control his anxiety enquired the reason to which Tenāli replied, "You see, neither I have done any miracle to drive away that putrid smell nor have you diluted your tannin solution. Simply, during this brief period, the seth had just become accustomed to the tan-yard's rotten smell."

The tanner smiled and nodded. Tenāli had been plainly waiting for the day the seth would get used to the repulsive smell emanating from the tannery and stop bothering the poor tanner. That was why he had made the tanner ask the seth to wait in the first place.

Once again Tenāli protected King Rāya's prestige with his brilliance and wit.

Life's Lesson

"Empathy is the cornerstone of all communication. Empathy is not only the ability to put yourself in the other's shoes and see his point of view. Wise people have empathy, therefore, they can get done more than most of the others."

Wise Cracks

☼ To get adapted to the changes is necessary for survival.

☼ Changes hit hard on our attitude and behaviour but certainly lead to new ideas and improvements.

Quotable Nugget

"Change is not made without inconvenience, even from worse to better."

Samuel Johnson

The Wish List

One fine morning, after laying siege to Udayagiri Fort for which the campaign lasted for a year, King Krishnadeva Rāya was sitting in his palace in a generous mood.

"Ask for anything and I'll give it to you," he said to the ashtadiggajas who had distinguished themselves in the tense moments during war.

"I always wanted to have a house in Vijayawada," excitedly said Thimmana, one of the ashtadiggajas.

"Done!" said the King, "you'll surely get a mansion in Vijayawada."

"I always desired to own an Inn in the temple city of Tirupati," said Dhurjati, another ashtadiggaja.

"Centre of excellence"

"Done!" said the Emperor. "I'll order an Inn to be given to you."

So, the other ashtadiggajas also desired to have either an orchard or an eatery or a countryside bungalow for which assurances were given by the King for fulfilment.

"And you, Sir?" the King finally asked Tenāli Raman. "What will you have?"

"Grant me a fortnight's leave," said Tenāli instantly.

"Done!" said King Krishnadeva, "Your leave begins from tomorrow!"

Now, Tenāli happened to be an eminent luminary of Bhuvana Vijayam, so his colleague ashtadiggajas were surprised to note as to why Tenāli had asked for so little. They felt that Tenāli had missed a rare opportunity to become rich but were elated to keep their wits by asking valuable things from the King. The ashtadiggajas asked Tenāli about his strange demand when they ran into him later that day.

"Why did you make a request so small?" they taunted Tenāli. "Did courage fail you?"

"You asked for a lot," replied Tenāli. "But you must remember that our Emperor is a busy man. He will just order his Prime Minister to fulfil his promises given to you. The Prime Minister too is an action-packed busy man. He will pass on the orders to his secretary or assistant for compliance who too are busy men. So, the Emperor's order will trickle down from subordinate to subordinate and finally in the course of few months . . . all will get lost eventually!"

"In that case, we'll appeal to the Emperor!" shouted Thimmana.

"The Emperor will not know what you all are talking about," said Tenāli. "By that time our great victory would have become a history with a dim memory. You should have asked for something that the Emperor could have given you instantaneously – like what I did. Now, if you'll excuse me gentlemen, I have lot of work to do."

And leaving the courtiers gaping, Tenāli went off to arrange for his holiday.

LIFE'S LESSON

"Those who are happiest, are ones who take care of TODAY. Many live in the past, or worry about the future. They forget that 'today is the day, we worried about yesterday — and it did not happen!"

Wise Cracks

- ☼ Whatever you want to do, do it now! There are only so many tomorrows.
- ☼ Seize today, and put as little trust as you can in tomorrow.
- ☼ A promise loses its sheen with time.
- ☼ Time dilutes the essence of needs and desires.
- ☼ It is worthwhile to make promises or contracts for things which are handy or readily available.

Quotable Nugget

"Defer not till tomorrow to be wise, tomorrow's sun to thee may never rise."

William Congreve

"Vows made in storms are forgotten in calms."

English Proverb

The Striking Questions

Once, while undertaking a tour to Bijapur to appraise the state of affairs, King Krishnadeva Rāya came across a village where he witnessed an extravagant marriage ceremony thrown by an affluent landlord of the village.

The King wanting to test Tenāli Raman's intelligence asked him, "Can you guess how much the landlord might have spent on that wedding?"

"About the cost of three sacks of rice and two sacks of wheat," said Tenāli.

The King's mouth dropped open in amazement. "The cost of three sacks of rice and two sacks of wheat!" he wondered. "Don't be thoughtless Tenāli; the landlord might have spent a fortune on the wedding!"

"Macro thinking"

Tenāli said nothing.

"Tenāli is an imprudent person," thought the King.

A few weeks later, while they were again undertaking a tour of Udayagir, they met with a funeral procession.

"Who has died?" asked the King, stopping a mourner. "Is it just one corpse or a hundred?" asked Tenāli. The King, greatly embarrassed by Tenāli's question, rode away without waiting for the mourner's answer.

Soon they came upon some labourers working in the paddy fields. "Looks like you had a good harvest!" asked the King to a peasant mowing the land.

"But are you reaping this year's harvest or last year's?" interrupted Tenāli. The King was staggered at such a question from Tenāli.

Back at the Royal Palace, the King discussed the entire episode with Nandi Timmanna, a literary luminary and one of the ashtadiggajas of the Bhuvana Vijayam and said, "Tenāli Ramalinga is a thoughtless person. He is falsely called the Kumara Bharathi and Vikatakavi!"

"Thoughtless! But Tenāli is noted for his brilliance and wit, My Lord. Before drawing any conclusion, why don't you give an opportunity to Tenāli and ask him to explain his silly questions."

The King did not say anything. But later when he found himself alone with Tenāli, he decided to act on Timmanna's advice.

"Tell me Tenāli," the King said pensively, "on seeing the funeral procession, what did you mean when you asked the mourner whether they were carrying one corpse or a hundred?"

"Some men have scores of dependents," explained Tenāli. "When such a man dies, many lives are shattered. His devastated dependents die with him, in a way. That is why I asked the mourner whether they were carrying one corpse or a hundred."

"Then what did you mean when you asked those labourers whether they were harvesting this year's crop or last year's?" asked the King thoughtfully.

"Despite our compelling efforts, most of these labourers are perennially in debt," explained Tenāli, "I was enquiring whether they were working to pay off last year's debt or had paid it all and were beginning anew."

The King now realised that his court jester, too far from being a nitwit, was probably cleverer than he has ever thought.

"One last question Tenāli," the King said. "The other day on our tour to Bijapur, why did you say that the landlord had spent only the equivalent of the price of three sacks of rice and two sacks of wheat for the wedding, when you knew fully well that the wedding was a lavish one?"

"What the landlord spent on the essentials of the marriage amounted to only a few varahas (gold coins)," smiled Tenāli. "The rest he spent was to uphold and enhance his prestige. In other words, he spent not on the marriage but on himself."

Hearing this, the King realised that there is no match for Tenāli Raman's wit and intellect.

Life's Lesson

"You need to see, not just look. You need to listen, not just hear. You need to go beyond the obvious. That is the mark of a great mind and a wise man."

Wise Cracks

- ☼ Nothing is more difficult than to be able to judge a person's intelligence.
- ☼ Judgement about a person's intelligence is not a superficial activity, it requires insight into the character and events.
- ☼ It is only shallow people who judge by appearances.

Quotable Nugget

Knowledge is the treasure, but judgement is the treasure of a wise man.

An
Ugly Truth

$\mathcal{D}$uring King Krishnadeva Rāya's reign, all poets, scholars and philosophers were widely patronised.

One day in the Imperial Palace, an intense argument arose between Thathacharya, the Rajaguru and Madayagari Mallanna, one of the ashtadiggajas.

During the argument, Mallanna held boldly, "Rajaguru, it is very easy to find a fault in others but it is a really difficult task to improve one's your faults. Everybody should endeavour to make improvements."

"I disagree with you, Mallanna," the Rajaguru said confidently.

"Unhealthy acts"

Tenāli Raman was watchfully listening to their arguments from a distance. While all this was happening, a lean man entered the Bhuvana Vijayam. He respectfully bowed in front of the King and introducing himself to the King said, "Your Highness, my name is Srinu Vaitla and I am a painter from the temple city of Sringeri. I have made various paintings during my life time such as that of Dasavathara (ten avatars of Vishnu) and Girijakalyana (marriage of goddess Parvati) amongst many others. I have brought a grand specimen especially for you. This stunning painting took me several years to complete." Saying this, Srinu Vaitla showed the magnificent painting to the King.

The King took the painting from Srinu Vaitla. The painting was that of a gorgeous woman. It was a fabulous piece of art and looked real. The King showed the painting to all his ashtadiggajas and the courtiers.

But surprisingly each of them seeing the painting found something wrong in the painting. Everyone in the court criticised the painting. According to some, the lady's cheeks were sunken; some said that her nose was too large while others criticised her hair. Still some others found defect with her eyes and eyebrows.

Thus, all courtiers found fault with the painting and criticised it vehemently.

Now it was Tenāli Raman's turn to give his comments on the painting. After fixing his eyes on the painting for a while, Tenāli said softly, "Your Majesty, I am not a good art critic. Therefore, in order to have a right viewpoint on Srinu's work, I am of the opinion that this painting should be hanged at the city's crossroads and an announcement should be made that anyone who observes a fault or an error in the painting can mark that error on the painting itself. In this way, you can have the exact comments from the people."

The King liked the proposal. He ordered his men to hang the painting on a pole at the city's crossroads. According to the King's orders, an announcement was also made in Hampi that everyone was free to mark faults or errors on the painting.

After a few days, the painting was brought back to the Royal Court in front of the King, and his ashtadiggajas and courtiers. The painting was a great mess and in a total disorder. The markings by the people had hidden the face of the lady in the painting.

The King was puzzled to see the painting in a chaos. Once again Tenāli recommended, "My Lord, let the painting be hanged once again at the city's crossroads and an announcement be made that those who had marked the faults on the painting must now improve upon them. For this, they will be rewarded suitably."

Once again the painting was hung at the city's crossroads. This time, no one came forward to rectify the faults which they had marked.

After a few days, the painting was brought back to the King. He saw that it was still a mess. Tenāli Raman said, "Your Highness, this is a bitter truth. As a common human nature, everyone of us is ever ready to find faults and defects in others but we are never ready to put them right."

Saying so, Tenāli glanced at Mallanna who understood that Tenāli was supporting his view. Tenāli explained his standpoint without hurting the feelings of Rajaguru who however felt humiliated at his defeat.

LIFE'S LESSON

"Look at the mole in your own eye, before pointing out the mole in your neighbour's eye — says the Bible. 'Physician — heal thyself' is an old adage.

'He has the right to criticise, who has the heart to help', said Lincoln.

Lesson for all of us — in these single line directives."

Wise Cracks

- ☼ It's easier to point out faults but difficult to remove them.
- ☼ We know that limitations exist in all. A bird can roost on only one branch.
- ☼ A mouse can drink no more than its fill even from a river.

Quotable Nuggets

"Men cease to interest us when we find their limitations."

Ralph Waldo Emerson

"Criticism is easy, art is difficult."

Derrouches

Twinkle in
Wrinkle

$\mathcal{T}$ax levies on personal income and land revenue formed the main source of revenue for Vijayanagara Empire. King Krishnadeva Rāya maintained well-functioning administrative methods for proper tax governance.

For tax collection, the empire was divided into five main Rajyas (provinces) which were sub-divided into Kottams (regions). These were further divided into Nadus (counties) which were again subdivided into Sthalas (municipalities). To facilitate tax administration at the lowest level, a separate Niyoga (department) was assigned with the function of tax collection duly supervised by Goudas (feudal landlords) and Karanikas (accountants).

All taxpayers of the empire were cautiously listed by the authorities regularly. Tenāli Raman always topped this list of taxpayers owing to massive

"Jewel in the crown"

126

rewards conferred upon him by the King, which also formed a part of his taxable income.

The names of other prominent functionaries such as Mahapradhana (Prime Minister), Pradhanas (cabinet of ministers), Karyakartha (Chief Secretary) and Adhikaris (Imperial Officers) followed his name in the list.

Once, Thathacharya (the Rajaguru) and a few envious courtiers showing the list of taxpayers told the King, "Tenāli draws less salary than most of other prime courtiers but his name always appears at the top of the taxpayers' list. His sources of income seem to be large which is questionable."

The King knew that the rewards which Tenāli gets on the occasions of his displaying acts of intelligence were also a prominent source of income. Anyhow taking note of the Rajaguru's and courtiers' contention, the King considered to give a fair chance to Tenāli to explain his position and ordered the Royal Attendant to fetch Tenāli Raman in the Bhuvana Vijayam the next day.

Tenāli Raman came to know of this entire episode from his faithful colleagues.

Next day Tenāli arrived late at the Royal Court with a jute bag hanging by his shoulder. The bag was stuffed and lively.

Greeting the King, Tenāli said, "Your Honour, I beg your pardon for coming to the Royal Court a bit late. Actually, this cock has become a persistent problem for me and it is the sole reason for my delay today," Tenāli paused taking a fat oversized cock out of his bag.

"How?" the King demanded an explanation from Tenāli.

"Sir, I have raised this cock and ten hens at my home. Everyday, I put twenty grams of chicken feed in the cage (pen) for each bird with the hope that each of the bird in the cage would get its share of feed. Unfortunately, this mischievous cock alone gulps up the maximum of the feed leaving the poor hens hungry and deprived. Please suggest a solution for this naughty cock?" exclaimed Tenāli pensively.

The King grinned and said, "You don't want to do anything. This cock is in the pink of its health and thus is the ruler of the cage. It will eat as per its body size. The cock is not to be blamed." Hearing this, Tenāli put the cock in its bag.

The King coming to discuss the business issues said, "Tenāli! Today, you have been called for to explain that though you earn less salary as compared to other courtiers, yet you are the highest taxpayer every year. What is the reason behind your huge money?"

Tenāli Raman chuckled and said, "Your Honour, I showed you how my devil cock gulps the extra feed. Similarly, I am the lone cock in your flock of hens."

Hearing Tenāli's explanation, the King laughed and so did the entire court leaving the envious courtiers embarrassed.

Life's Lesson

"Top performers and achievers will always be surrounded by envy and jealousy. It is only natural. But if there is obvious proof that such performers are effective and efficient and deliver, all such murmurs will get muted."

Wise Cracks

- ☼ Men are not superior by race or colour, but by heart and brain.
- ☼ Educated and wise men are as much superior to uneducated men as the living are to the dead.
- ☼ There are three marks of a superior man; being virtuous, he is free from anxiety; being wise, he is free from perplexity; being brave, he is free from fear.

Quotable Nugget

"It is the mark of a superior man that, left to himself, he is able endlessly to amuse, interest and entertain himself out of his personal stock of meditations, ideas, criticisms, memories, philosophy, humour and what not."

George Jean Nathan

The 'Son'shine

King Krishnadeva Rāya had a very grand and picturesque garden in his palace. The garden had a wide variety of flowers planted in it which included some rare species fetched from distant places. The King was very particular towards the upkeep of his royal garden and used to take personal care of it. The King had deployed Kavalus (special guards) for its close vigil and maintenance.

Though the King liked each and every plant of his garden but amongst the wide assortment of flowers, he had special affinity for a rose climber, which was gifted to him by a European traveller namely, Fernao Nuniz. The climber used to bear very fragrant and magnificent flowers.

"A teacher, speaker and a preacher all the way"

The King used to take a daily stroll in the royal garden and enjoy the splendid view of the blossoming plants and their fragrance.

One day, during his usual stroll in the royal garden, the King observed that the rose climber was not bearing flowers properly. He immediately called for the Adhikari (Imperial Officer) responsible for the upkeep of the royal garden and asked him, "This climber is not blossoming as usual. It is not yielding the quantity of flowers it is supposed to. I think some miscreant is stealing the flowers from this climber. Keep a close check over the royal garden and be more watchful. Best efforts should be made for its close watch."

Hearing the King's strict orders, the Adhikari of the royal garden deployed extra Kavalus and intensified patrolling around the garden 24X7 to keep a close check over it. Despite such efforts, the thief could not be caught.

One early morning when the sun was about to rise, a little boy cautiously entered the garden and hurriedly started plucking flowers from plants including that specific rose climber. The Kavalus on duty caught sight of the mischievous lad plucking and tugging the flowers hastily. The Kavalus at once came into action and leaped over the boy and caught him red-handed with a bunch of brilliant flowers and took him to the Adhikari.

The Adhikari instantly informed the King about the thief. Within minutes, the news of nabbing the thief who stole flowers from the royal garden spread all over Hampi.

At daybreak, the jubilant Adhikari and the Kavalus led a procession of the boy throughout Hampi to exhibit their success in nabbing the thief.

Listening to the intense commotion on the city's streets, Tenāli Raman came out of his home and saw his son being carried away by the royal guards. His wife also seeing the boy being taken to the royal court wept and pleaded Tenāli to to get her dear son released.

As the guards holding the boy crossed him, Tenāli screamed, "The boy is caught red-handed with the bunch of flowers in his possession. He had done a crime for which he will be severely punished beyond any doubt. But, if the boy has sharp teeth and tongue, he can be saved from the punishment. All he has to do is to realise his having sharp teeth and tongue to use them at the right moment."

While the boy heard his father's words, he thought that his father is a bright person and never speaks worthless words. Every word of his father has a deep meaning hidden within it and these words might also have some definite message and meaning for him.

Pondering for a while, the little boy got hold of the clue. He was holding the bunch of flowers he had plucked from the royal garden. Gradually, the boy started munching the tender flowers unnoticed. When the guards and the boy reached the Royal Court, the boy had already eaten away all the flowers and he was empty-handed.

The Adhikari presented the little boy before the King and said, "Your Majesty, here is the thief who had made our nights sleepless and had kept the royal guards on their toes. This thief should be severely punished for his crime."

Hearing this, the timid boy roared, "Your Highness, I am not a thief at all. They just caught hold of me because they failed to catch the real culprit. You can even get me thoroughly searched. I don't have any flowers in my possession. These guards are a pack of liars."

The King immediately ordered the guards and attendants to thoroughly search the little boy. The guards obeyed the orders of the King but were astonished not to find a single flower from the boy. They knew that the boy had definitely stolen the flowers. But now they could not prove themselves due to lack of any evidence in support of the guilt of the boy.

The King yelled at the guards, "You all are careless and hasty. You have just wasted the court's precious time. You have neither caught any thief nor provided any evidence in support of your claim. I cannot punish anybody on the basis of your false claims. This little boy should be released immediately. And you all be more careful and vigilant in future towards discharge of your duties."

Tenāli Raman's son was released because of the total effenct of the 'father-son' duo, their intelligence and presence of mind. The boy came back to home cheerfully.

Life's Lesson

"Quick thinking - fast execution - excellent coordination. All these got the culprit 'off the hook'. But the question remains. Was this the right thing to do? Did not the wrongdoing deserve the required punishment? Did this incident show that blood is thicker than water?"

Wise Cracks

☼ Strategy without tactics is the slowest route to victory and tactics without strategy is the noise before defeat.

☼ Without tactics you can learn nothing.

☼ Tactics teaches you when to be silent and when and how to come to actions.

Quotable Nugget

"To be meek, patient, tactful, modest, honourable, brave, is not to be either manly or womanly; it is to be humane."

Jane Harrison

The Rich Versus
The Poor

"The poor people are more dishonest as compared to rich. The poor are deceitful owing to their poverty and are the sole cause of all thefts and crimes in the Kingdom," contended Thathacharya (the Rajaguru) in the Bhuvana Vijayam one day.

Tenāli Raman objected to this abrupt opinion of the Rajaguru and requested King Krishnadeva Rāya to give him a chance to prove his view. Tenāli requested the King for two bags each containing fifty varahas (gold coins) and a month's time.

The King agreed to Tenāli's suggestion.

"Man of the moment"

After a few days, Tenāli Raman dropped a bag containing the varahas on a lonely path passing through a dense forest and hid himself behind a tree to witness the happening. Soon, a rich trader passed by. He saw the bag containing the varahas. He immediately grabbed it and thinking it to be his destiny, took the bag home and hid it.

A little later, Tenāli dropped the second bag of varahas on the same path and hid himself behind a tree. After a while, a poor man happened to pass through the path and saw the bag lying unattended on the path. The poor man picked up the bag and thought that someone might have lost it. He further thought that the real owner must be quite worried of having lost his bag, so the bag should be deposited with the royal treasury to make it reach its real owner.

The poor man went straight to the royal treasury and deposited the bag.

Tenāli Raman had secretly observed the entire episode. Next day, he went to the Bhuvana Vijayam and narrated the entire episode to the King and the courtiers. Tenāli told the King that only one bag had been deposited in the royal treasury and that too by the poor man.

The next morning, both the rich and the poor men were called in the Bhuvana Vijayam. King Rāya asked the rich trader, "The other day you found a bag full of varahas lying unattended on the path. Where is that bag?"

"Your Honour, I had invested the money in my business as I have recently suffered a great loss," said the trader.

"But that bag was not yours . . . then how come you have invested the money in your business?" inquired the King. "Your Honour, I thought it was my sheer luck and took it to be a blessing from Goddess Lakshmi," the trader responded.

Then the King asked the poor man, "Why did you deposit the bag with the royal treasury? You are a poor person, you might have used it."

"Your Honour, that money did not belonged to me. I thought that the real owner might be worried about his lost bag and would be in more need than me. My principles and morality did not allow me to keep the money which is not mine," replied the poor man.

Hearing the views of the rich and the poor man, Tenāli Raman said assertively, "Your Honour, this clearly shows that the poor man is truthful and the rich man is rather dishonest."

The King and the courtiers agreed with Tenāli's opinion and the Rajaguru felt ashamed.

LIFE'S LESSON

"Honesty and levels of wealth are not mutually exclusive. One can be rich or poor and yet be honest. The rich are cooks and the poor are needy — and both cannot be trusted — are hooks are used by us, to hang over menial 'types'."

Wise Cracks

- ☼ No habit is as rich as honesty. It is the best guideline.
- ☼ An honest man is said to be the noblest work of God.
- ☼ It is better to be poor than to be dishonest.
- ☼ Peace depends on honesty.
- ☼ He who has lost his honesty has nothing more to lose.

Quotable Nugget

"A heavy purse makes a light heart."

Anonymous

Cup of
Woes

$\mathcal{A}$t the time of King Krishnadeva Rāya's accession to the throne, the condition of Vijayanagara Empire was unstable. The King had to deal simultaneously with rebellious subordinates and aggression of Northern Muslim Kingdoms, the hostility of the Gajapatis of Orissa and the annual jihadi onslaught from the Bahamani Kingdom. The entire Empire had to face these adversaries loyally and vigilantly to come out successfully. In short, the situation was distressing and offensive.

During such worrying period, once the King and the courtiers got together for a sharbat session at the Royal Palace. All the scholarly luminaries of the Vijayanagara Empire sat across discussing the obstacles being persistently faced by the Empire. The situation of the Kingdom was very stressful and there was nothing to provide relief.

To offer hospitality, the King had ordered to serve sharbat and snacks to all the guests. Just when the sharbat and snacks were about to be served,

"Highs and lows"

Tenāli Raman got up from the assembly and went straight to the royal kitchen only to return with a large jug of sharbat and an assortment of glasses – porcelain, terracotta, glass, crystal, gold, silver, copper glasses – some plain looking, some expensive, some exquisite – telling the guests to help themselves to the sharbat.

When all the guests had a glass of sharbat each in their hands, Tenāli said, "If you notice, all the nice-looking expensive cups were taken up, leaving behind the plain and cheap ones. While it is normal for us to want only the best of ourselves, that is the source of our problems and stress." He continued, "what all of us wanted was sharbat, not the glass, but we consciously opted for the best glasses and were eyeing each other's glasses. Now consider this: Life is the sharbat and the success, positions and money are the glasses. They are just tools to hold and contain life and do not change the quality of life. Sometimes, by concentrating only on the glass, we fail to enjoy the life which has been provided to us. So, we should try not to be enchanted by glasses, don't get driven by that. We should endeavour to enjoy the sharbat or life."

Listening to these words of Tenāli Raman, the King and the courtiers felt quite relieved of the tremendous pain and burden posed by the gruelling state of affairs.

Life's Lesson

"In the rush and tumble of life and our involvement in social and professional milieu, we often fail to distinguish style from substance. Those who are wise and happy – are those who focus on substance."

Wise Cracks

- ☼ Life is running from want to want, not from enjoyment to enjoyment.
- ☼ The fewer our wants, the happier we are.
- ☼ The secret of all success is to know how to govern ourselves and obey the command of our own conscience.
- ☼ Most powerful is he who has himself in his own power and has a watchful eye over his own wants and deeds.

Quotable Nugget

"How few our real wants, and how vast our imaginary ones."

Lavater

Of The People, For The People, By The People

King Krishnadeva Rāya used to undertake frequent tours of his vast empire and hear grievances of the people to redress them then and there itself. Once while passing through Vijayawada with his entourage, King Krishnadeva Rāya asked Tenāli Raman, "Who do you think is the greatest man?"

Tenāli said, "Without doubt, you are the greatest, for you are a King who commands many men and has triumphed in all the wars you have waged. You are the 'Kannadaraya' – the greatest statesman which Deccan has ever produced."

The King continued, "Who do you think is greater than me?"

"It has to be the Vijayanagara Empire; the glorious kingdom in the South : extending from Cuttack in east to Goa in the west, and from Raichur Doab in the north to the Indian Ocean in the south," asserted Tenāli.

"Son of the soil"

"Now take me to him who is greater than the Vijayanagara Empire and me put together," desired the King.

Both the King and Tenāli travelled further till they came upon a man who was all alone digging a well.

"Here he is,." Said Tenāli, "a man greater than both the King and the most flourished empire taken together. Patiently, and all by himself, he is digging a well, not that he shall have drinking water from the well but others will be benefitted from it. Only he can be called the greatest person who spends his life in the service of others, with no expectation of reward or benefit to himself."

Listening to Tenāli's reply, the King nodded his head in agreement, and decided and endeavoured to relentlessly and selflessly serve his subjects with better administrative reforms.

Life's Lesson

"The Bible calls them 'the salt of the earth'. They are those who spend their life in the service of others. They are people like Mother Teresa and Baba Amte. They help to make this a better world — and they leave the world richer, than when they came into it."

Wise Cracks

- ☼ Hard work and selfless labour conquers everything.
- ☼ Selfless labour is the source of peace and pleasure.
- ☼ There is no real wealth but unselfish labour of man. Without sincere labour nothing prospers.
- ☼ Capital is only condensed labour.
- ☼ Real wealth comes to the man who has learned that he is paid best for the things he does for nothing.

Quotable Nugget

"The bee is more honoured than other animals, not because she labours, but because she labours for others."

St. John Chrysostom

"The man who holds the ladder at the bottom is frequently of more service than the man at the top."

Anonymous.

Search
Simplified

One morning when King Krishnadeva Rāya was seated in the Bhuvana Vijayam discussing issues of State governance with his courtiers, a group of young boys entered the Royal Court followed by an elderly man. The group was stranger since no one had ever seen them before. They were exactly five boys in all, identically dressed and of same height and age. The courtiers thought them to be identical brothers.

Every courtier looked at them strangely.

The elderly man who had accompanied the five young boys was from Vellore. He walked straight to the King to make a request, "Your Highness, I have heard a lot about the wit and intelligence of the Royal Court. Can anyone in your Court solve a peculiar problem for me and give me the correct answer?"

"State of turmoil"

"What is your problem?" asked the King strangely.

"By just looking at these five young boys, you have to tell me which of them is the prince of Vellore," said the elderly man.

"Your Ruler might be quite bright to have thought of such a puzzle for my Court," said the King joyfully. "I understand that we shall be quite lucky to furnish you the right answer. But someone here might already know how the prince looks like? Then it wouldn't be much of a problem," continued the King.

The elderly man giggled and told the King, "It's not so simple. I had already made sure that no one of your Court knew how the real prince of Vellore looks like. It's only after verifying that I have brought the boys here and asked such a question."

"Well, we shall try if anyone in my Court is able to provide you with the precise answer," said King Rāya.

"Your Honour, let us call the royal astrologer," suggested the ashtadiggaja Dhurjati, "he will be able to tell the real prince by reading the boys' palms."

"Or simply ask them a few questions," said another ashtadiggaja Rama Bhadrudu, "the way a prince speaks and answers is quite different from the way others do. So, it would be easy to figure out the real prince."

"No... That is not allowed," said the elderly man straightaway. "No one is to speak to them or see their palms. You have to identify the prince by just looking at the boys. That's all."

"That's a very difficult task to determine the real prince from the group who are identical?" the courtiers agreed.

Seeing all courtiers failing to provide an answer, the King confidently requested Tenāli Raman to examine the problem and solve it.

Obeying the King's orders, Tenāli Raman stood from his seat and walked out of the Court and after a while returned carrying a packet of modakas (a sweetmeat of Deccan region made of condensed milk and flour) in his hand. He walked up straight to the boys and said, "Please have a modaka each before doing anything else. I am sure you might be hungry."

Four of the boys grabbed the modakas from Tenāli's hand but the fifth boy stood silently.

"You too have a modaka," persuaded Tenāli.

But the boy looked at Tenāli's face without uttering a word and did not take the modaka.

Tenāli smiled and took him by the hand and led him to the King, "Your Honour, he is the prince of Vellore."

"Is Tenāli's answer right?" asked the King.

"Yes, he is absolutely right," said the elderly man smilingly, "but may I ask how Tenāli did it?"

"Will you tell us how you picked out the real prince, Tenāli?" asked the King, "all of us are eager to know how you did it."

"It's quite simple, Your Honour," said Tenāli cheerfully, "people who belong to royal families are used to give things to strangers but not accept things from strangers. Also, they are used to have everything done for them by their attendants, even when it comes to the basic activities of eating or drinking. Here also, the prince simply could not understand that he was being asked to take the modaka with his own hands. His lack of ability to react to the situation made it quite simple for me to recognise him. That's all."

King Rāya was pleased with Tenāli's wit and praised him heartily.

Life's Lesson

"All human beings are product of nature and nurture. A wise man is able to assess both when looking at a stranger. His assessment is therefore logical and credible, rather than a mere 'first impression'."

Wise Cracks

- ☼ Human nature is often hidden, sometimes comes out but is seldom extinguished.
- ☼ Human nature is the same everywhere; only the modes are different.
- ☼ It's easier to understand human nature keeping in mind that almost everybody thinks he's an exception to most rules when infact he is not.
- ☼ A creative and wise person with artistry to touch and move people, succeeds to understand every human nature.

Quotable Nugget

"Human nature may be an infinitely variant thing. But it has constants. One is that, given a choice, people keep what is the best for themselves."

John Kenneth Galbraith

A Landmark Victory

*R*amachandram Naidu of Talikota was a distinguished scholar having a remarkable command over all Shastras and Sutras. Unable to face the intellect of Naidu during debates, the scholars in many kingdoms acknowledged their defeat. After several triumphs, he came to the Kingdom of Vijayanagara with a desire to defeat the reputed ashtadiggajas of the Bhuvana Vijayam. King Krishnadeva Rāya, a great patron of literature agreed to hold a grand debate to judge the intellect of the scholars. After deciding the date of the debate, Ramachandram Naidu returned home.

Hearing about the triumphs and titles of Ramachandram Naidu, the eminent literary luminaries and poets of the Royal Court like Allasani Peddana, Nandi Timmanna and Kumara Dhurjati having notable proficiency in Telugu and Sanskrit

"Leaders lead the way"

scriptures hesitated to participate in the debate scheduled with Ramachandram Naidu. However, there was no other way out but to participate.

Baffled with the situation, Peddana and others together came to Tenāli Raman and said, "Tenāli Raman! This time too you have to save the honour of the ashtadiggajas and the Vijayanagara Empire. See that we don't lose our name and fame."

If Naidu is not defeated, the hard-earned prestige of the ashtadiggajas would be all gone. Realising this fact, Tenāli Raman thought of defeating Ramachandram Naidu.

The next day, Ramachandram Naidu came to Hampi for the debate and stayed in the Royal Guest House. Tenāli Raman also went to the Royal Guest House pretending to be a student of the Gurukulashram and sat outside waiting. Meanwhile, Ramachandram Naidu came out after his dinner and started strolling up and down.

On sighting Ramachandram Naidu, Tenāli Raman read out a beautiful poem.

After listening to the striking poem, Ramachandram Naidu was left spellbound at the literary contents of the poem recited by the disciple. Fascinated with the talent of the disciple, Naidu approached him and asked, "Who are you? What are you doing sitting here?"

"Nothing much, Sir! I am a disciple of Tenāli Raman, the scholar of the Imperial Court. I have been waiting here for a fellow student. My teacher Tenāli needs a book on logic to prepare for a debate scheduled for tomorrow in the Royal Court. While on my way to get the book, I rested here waiting for the other fellow. If I have disturbed you, I shall go away Sir," saying this modestly Tenāli got up.

Ramachandram Naidu interrupted him, "No, no. I enquired because I just wanted to know who you were. What is your teacher doing at present?"

"Sir, a celebrated scholar has come from Talikota to the Royal Court. My teacher has been chosen by the King and others to engage in a debate with the scholar. Now he must be going through several scriptures for that very purpose," he said and left.

On listening this, Ramachandram Naidu told himself, "What a surprise? If Tenāli Raman's disciple himself is so talented and versatile, Raman must certainly be a profound scholar. Without realising his worth, I came all the way and boasted in the Court. Let me escape now without facing a public humiliation." Ramachandram Naidu got up early the next morning and left Vijayanagara before daybreak.

Next morning, the news of Naidu's leaving Hampi spread like wildfire which rejoiced everybody because Tenāli Raman's cleverness again succeeded in saving the honour of Vijayanagar Empire.

Life's Lesson

"Most people spend a lot of time fighting their fears. They indulge in 'shadow boxing'. There is a fear of the unknown and what may happen. They forget the proven advice of the sages.

'Today is the day, we worried about yesterday – and it did not happen'."

Wise Cracks I

☼ Fear is the proof of a degenerated mind. It is a permanent emotion of the inferior man.
☼ Half of our fears are baseless and the other half discreditable.
☼ Fear of fear is more than the fear itself. So, it is great to live through life, without fear.

Quotable Nugget

"Fear is the most paralysing of all emotions. It can stiffen the muscles and stupefy the mind and the will."

Anonymous

Wise Cracks II

☼ Hasty decisions purely based on instinct are risky.
☼ A leader has to combine creative thinking with composite judicial thinking in arriving at decisions.
☼ Hurried decisions without actually facing the situation or without scanning the environment are not good decisions and make one lose valuable opportunities.

Quotable Nugget

"We ought to weigh well what we can only once decide."

Publilius Syrus

Under
Cover

 $\mathcal{T}$enāli Raman – the Vikatakavi was thought to possess immense wealth because of the repeated rewards and gifts bestowed upon him by King Krishnadeva Rāya. People took him to be utterly rich and understood that his house might be full of luxurious articles, jewellery and money. Thieves often thought their work would yield rich profits if they broke into Tenāli's house.

One night a poor thief, unable to dig a hole and get into Tenāli Raman's house, thought of stealing things by a clever trick. The thief thought he would enter Tenāli's house only at midnight under complete darkness. Meanwhile, he will hide himself somewhere in the bushes. He intended to come out after people in the house had eaten and slept, and to slip away with the booty effortlessly. With this preparation, the thief arrived early and sat stealthily in the bushes in the backyard of Tenāli Raman's house.

"Combative, passionate"

In the evening, as soon as Tenāli came home from the Royal Court, he spotted a human face in the bushes. Guessing rightly about the identity of the man to be a thief, Tenāli decided to play a trick on the fellow. He sat on the terrace and talked with the passerby for a long time and pretended as if he did not notice the thief hidden in the bushes. After a while, Tenāli Raman's wife reminded him that it was the time for dinner and handed him a towel so that he could bathe.

Tenāli Raman put off his Court attire, tied the towel around his waist, ready for bath and asked his wife to keep the hot water close to the bushes in which the thief was hiding.

The lady placed the water cauldron (bucket) near the bushes and kept handing him water in a small vessel (pitcher). Tenāli Raman kept on chatting with his wife, gargling and spitting the water repeatedly onto the bushes aiming at the hidden thief.

The thief in the bushes sat without moving, tolerating all the spit and hot sprinkled water thinking he was unnoticed. Finally, all the water in the cauldron was finished. Tenāli Raman poured the last water from the vessel into his mouth, gargled and spattered it on his wife jokingly. The annoyed lady let out a cry at once, "Enough of your monkey business. You seem to turn childish day by day. You have drenched my clothes."

Tenāli Raman chuckled and said loudly, "For one mouthful of water, you got irritated and let out a hundred abuses. Poor fellow! I do not know which noble woman's son he is, but look at the gentleman in the bushes. I gargled a full bucket of water on his head and splattered hot water at him but he never let out even a word."

Listening to these words, the thief came out of the bushes and fell at Tenāli Raman's feet, begging for forgiveness.

Life's Lesson

"In all communication, there is a direct and indirect way, there is a courteous and discourteous way, there is an empathetic and non-emphathetic way. This needs training and practice but it is worth the effort, because then you will have more friends than enemies or professional rivals."

Wise Cracks

- ☼ Moral is simply what you feel good after, and immoral is what you feel bad after.
- ☼ Immoral acts of cheating, stealing or treachery should be dealt with an iron-hand and the practitioner should be taught lessons.
- ☼ The world is built on moral foundations and in the long run it is well with the good but is ill with the wicked.

Quotable Nugget

"Absolute morality is the regulation of conduct that pain shall not be inflicted."

Herbert Spencer

Dons
To Dust

$\mathcal{T}$he growing intimacy of King Krishnadeva Rāya with Tenāli Raman and the King's confidence built for his jester became a cause of envy for other courtiers.

Once, a few envious courtiers collectively pleaded to the King, "Your Majesty, be kind enough to provide us an opportunity to accompany you on your tours instead of Tenāli."

The King felt this request to be just. He assured to take them with him on his future tours.

"A commited maveric"

Once when the King was going on a tour in disguise to some villages to get firsthand experience of the states of the villages, he took along with him two other courtiers ignoring Tenāli Raman.

The King and his accompanying courtiers had disguised themselves as villagers. After wandering, they reached a farm in a village. They saw a few farmers gossiping nearby. They went near the farmers and asked for water to drink.

While the farmers offered them water, the King enquired, "Dear Brothers, is anybody in trouble in your village? Do you have any grievances against King Rāya?"

These questions put the farmers in suspicion that the strangers might be some adhikaris (Imperial Officers) of the King. They replied, "There is peace and prosperity in our village. All people are happy. They work hard the whole day and sleep blissfully at night. No one has any problem. King Rāya treats his subjects as his own children and hence there can be no reason for anybody to be unhappy with the King."

"And what do other villagers think about their King?" enquired the King further.

At this, an old farmer got up and pulled a thick sugarcane from nearby farm and brought it to the King. Showing the sugarcane to the King, the old farmer replied, "Sir, our King is very similar to this sugarcane."

King Rāya was stunned to hear his comparison with sugarcane. He could neither understand the contention of the old farmer, nor could he get hold of the villagers' opinion about their King.

The puzzled King asked his courtiers to explain the meaning of the statement of the old farmer.

Both the courtiers were astonished at the example. They did not know what to say. Gathering courage one of the courtiers replied, "My Lord! The old man means that our King is weak like this thick sugarcane which can be easily uprooted in one jolt whenever anybody so desires, as he pulled out this sugarcane."

The King considered the courtier's explanation and felt it reasonable. He got wild with rage and challenged the old farmer, "You perhaps don't recognise me, as to who am I?"

On hearing the furious words of the King, the old farmer started trembling. Instantly another old man who was listening to the entire episode came out of the nearby hut and said politely, "Sir, we have recognised you very well, but feel very sorry that your associates do not know you in reality. My colleague here wants to say that our King is soft and sweet like sugarcane for his subjects, but is severely hard and harsh on criminals, crooks and enemies." The old person completed his talk of illustrating it by a severe blow with the sugarcane on a nearby standing dog.

On concluding his speech, the old man threw away his robe and removed his false beard and moustache as well. The associates of the King instantly exclaimed, "So Tenāli Raman, you have been chasing us so far?"

Tenāli replied, "How could I give up the pursuit? If I had not followed you, you would have got these simple peasants killed with your unreasonable comments, besides creating a high tide of anger in the calm ocean like heart of our great King."

The King said, "You are right Tenāli. It is always painful to be in the company of fools. In future I shall never go out with anyone else."

When the other villagers learnt about King Rāya and Tenāli, a grand reception was accorded in their honour.

The King was overwhelmed with such affection from the villagers and their love for him. The courtiers hurt with the remarks of Tenāli brooded in a corner, while the witty Tenāli sat beside the King smiling softly.

Life's Lesson

"Sometimes it is necessary to disguise youself to get the 'real picture'. In normal circumstances people are influenced by your personality, power, status, wealth - so they tell you what you want to hear. It is only when you wear a 'cloak' that they may be brutally frank and tell you 'as it is'."

Wise Cracks

☼ One of the greatest accomplishments a man can attain is the power to comprehend the true meaning of the words and events.

☼ Successful communication is not only increasingly difficult, intricate and expensive, it is also increasingly important.

Quotable Nugget

"Conversation should be pleasant without scurrility, witty without affection, free without indecency, learned without conceitedness, novel without falsehood."

William Shakespeare

The
Phoenix Moment

Once Tenāli Raman borrowed money from King Krishnadeva Rāya to meet his personal requirements. Soon the time for repaying the money arrived. But Tenāli was still not in a position to repay the money. So he devised a plot in his mind to escape the liability of repaying the money to the King.

As per his ploy, Tenāli conveyed to the King his inability to attend the Bhuvana Vigayam for a few days due to his illness.

Noticing Tenāli's long absence from the royal affairs, the King decided to visit him personally. Next day, accompanied by a few courtiers, the King paid a visit to Tenāli's house.

He found Tenāli lying shrivelled on a bed wrapped in a blanket. Seeing his state, the King enquired the reason of Tenāli's illness from his wife.

"Breath of death"

She explained, "Your Honour, he has fallen ill because he is under your burden of debt."

The King was moved by these words and sympathetically said, "There's no need to worry. You are no longer bound to pay the debt. Don't be bothered now and be hale and hearty immediately."

On hearing these words, Tenāli jumped out of the bed. He grinned and shouted, "Thank you very much, Your Honour!"

The King asked surprisingly, "What's this? You were not ill. You told a lie to me by pretending to be ill!" The King got annoyed.

"No Sir, I didn't lie! I was ill under your burden of debt. Now that you have lifted the burden, I am healthy again."

Hearing Tenāli's words, the King was speechless.

Life's Lesson

"Pretence and crude dramatics may help you get out of an uncomfortable situation. But one must ask oneself. Is this really acceptable? Is it worth destroying long-term trust, to ensure short-term gains?"

Wise Cracks

- Debt is the worst poverty.
- There is no life in a family that depends on borrowing and debt.
- Debt brings the slavery to the free.
- Debts surely shorten life.

Quotable Nugget

"The second vice is by lying, the first is running into debt."

Benjamin Franklin

Acting Care-fooly

Once for some reasons the entire Vijayanagara Kingdom witnessed lots of mice. People were displeased to find mice everywhere spreading disease, leaving droppings, destroying foodgrains etc. They approached King Krishnadeva Rāya for a solution to the mice invasion.

Seeking suggestion from Thathacharya (the Rajaguru), the King proposed that each family should be given a cat which would solve the mice menace permanently. The family cat would keep a check on the mice. Further, in order to feed the cat and encourage cat-keeping, the King also ordered to give a sum of money every month to each house.

Everyone liked the idea but Tenāli Raman was not happy with the King's silly declaration causing undue burden on the royal treasury for a petty and natural issue.

"All for a good cause"

So a number of cats alongwith money from the royal treasury were distributed to all houses in the Kingdom. Like everyone, Tenāli also took a cat and money home.

After a few days, surprisingly it was observed that instead of decrease in the mice population, its number increased. Nothing happened despite a drain on royal treasury. Noticing this pattern, the King enquired why the cats were not helping to check the mice.

When the King came to know that the cats were infact not hunting mice, he ordered that each household should display its pet cat in the Bhuvana Vijayam.

The next day, the cats were examined in the Royal Court. All the cats were found to be in good health - plump and fleshy. In the end, the King called for the cat from Tenāli's house. Finding Tenāli's cat very thin, the King asked irritably, "The royal treasury is paying you a good sum of money every month, how come your cat is so weak and slender?"

Tenāli replied that he did not know why his cat never drank milk since the first day. The King and the Court were amazed. The King did not believe Tenāli's words. The King ordered the royal servant to bring a bowl of milk and give it to the cat. Immediately the cat jumped and ran away from the milk bowl.

Not understanding the reason, the King asked Tenāli to come open with the whole truth. Everyone in the Court wanted to know why Tenāli's cat would not even lick a drop of milk.

Tenāli said, "Your Honour, if we feed the cat stomach full with three meals everyday, why would it run after the mice? So, on the first day itself, I offered steaming hot milk to my cat. It got its tongue burnt. Now, it never drinks milk at our house. But it goes after the mice killing them and checking its population. The cat not only kills the mice but searches for bits of food here and there. And my house does not have this pest problem. The money which I got from the royal treasury was used for my household purposes."

The King came to his senses and he abandoned the entire scheme. He realised the undue burden on the royal treasury and his people also realised that the pest problem is just a natural phenomenon and they had to solve this problem on their own.

Life's Lesson

"Problems in the 'nature/environment' are best solved by solutions in this same environment. Most times these work. Nature is the world's finest and largest laboratory. Perhaps we have disturbed this to some extent by interfering with natural processes."

Wise Cracks

- ☼ Nature is not governed, except by obeying her.
- ☼ Nature is neutral and very comfortable with herself.
- ☼ Nature is the creation of God which never breaks her own laws.
- ☼ Those things are better which are perfected by nature than those which are finished by machines.

Quotable Nugget

"Nature does not proceed by leaps."

Carolus Linnaeus

The Bold One

Once in the Bhuvana Vijayam, King Krishnadeva Rāya and his courtiers were busy discussing issues regarding the welfare of the subjects.

During discussion, Tenāli Raman made a suggestion to an issue. Suddenly, some of the jealous courtiers laughed uncontrollably at Tenāli's suggestion.

This not only irritated Tenāli Raman but infuriated the King also.

Unexpectedly, Tenāli paused and facing towards the courtiers roared, "I am sorry to say this . . . but it's true that half of the scholars assembled here are foolish and clumsy people! It's very unfortunate that such fools are my colleagues."

This statement of calling the well-versed courtiers foolish by Tenāli Raman gave rise to an uproar and anger amongst the courtiers. The resentful courtiers requested the King to immediately punish Tenāli for such misbehaviour. When

"Towering pressure"

the anguish of the courtiers could not be controlled, the King and the Prime Minister Timmarusu intervened and advised Tenāli to take back his words and feel sorry for his rude comments.

Tenāli Raman being a submissive person agreed and in a sober tone remarked, "My fellow colleagues! I respect all of you and admire your intelligence. I feel sorry and take back my words . . . Half of you are not foolish," and saying this, Tenāli smilingly left the court.

The envious courtiers felt embarrassed and understood that Tenāli has again very cleverly and boldly made his point.

Life's Lesson

"Communicaiton is derived from the latin word 'communis' which means 'sharing of meaning'. Those who master art of communication not only use words, but also paralinguistics like tone and body language. They are then able to command the situation - and greatly influence other people."

Wise Cracks

- ☼ An important thing about any word is how you understand it.
- ☼ Words have immense power. A blow with a word strikes deeper than a blow with a sword.
- ☼ A well-chosen word can stop a moving army, to change defeat into victory, and to save an empire. Words rightly spoken are like apples of gold in pictures of silver.
- ☼ Without knowing the force of words, it is impossible to understand meaning.

Quotable Nugget

"It is with words as with sunbeams—the more they are condensed, the deeper they burn."

Robert Southey

Wanted:
An Urgent Solution

*O*nce, many people in Hampi became severely ill. All of them suffered from stomach ailments, severe pains, cramps and aches in the abdomen. The King got worried by such repeated reports.

After examining many patients, the Royal Physician reported to King Rāya that all people who suffered from stomach ailments have eaten powdered black pepper. On testing powdered black pepper, it was found to be containing stones and charcoal finely powdered and mixed with pepper. That made the people seriously ill.

The King was surprised to know the report. He became furious and announced that all shopkeepers selling powdered black pepper be arrested and put behind bars.

"Taking things to another level"

161

The King's orders were abided and all shopkeepers selling powdered black pepper were arrested and put behind bars. The cruel orders of the King made the relatives of the shopkeepers distressed. They pleaded the King to release their people but the infuriated King declined their requests. The shopkeepers would now be imprisoned rigorously for the crime they have not committed.

The relatives of shopkeepers got together and approached Tenāli Raman for help. They explained, "Our relatives are being punished for a crime which they have not committed. They were only selling powdered black pepper. It is the person who grinds the pepper and mixes it with powdered stones and charcoal. And that evil person is Rajaguru's brother who supplies this powdered black pepper to all the shops. Please do something for we have come to seek justice. Please suggest an urgent solution to this malady."

Tenāli assured them his help. Tenāli thought about the problem for a long time and soon went to the banks of the Tungabhadra River. He entered a small hut of a fisherman situated on the banks of the Tungabhadra River and began kicking at the earthen pots in which water had been stored. After that, he went into many such hutments and behaved in the similar manner. Soon the sounds of breaking the pots and pitchers attracted all the fishermen. When they saw Tenāli kicking and breaking their earthen pots full of water, they were horrified, "Please Tenāli stop! Please do not break our pots," they pleaded.

But Tenāli paid no heed to them. Soon the word spread that Tenāli Raman had gone mad. He was going from house to house breaking down earthen pots. This news reached King Rāya too. He got furious and worried too.

King Rāya rushed to the village of fishermen on the banks of Tungabhadra River. He saw Tenāli breaking the earthen pots. He said, "Stop Tenāli! Why are you behaving like a mad man? Why are you breaking all these pots?"

"Your Majesty!" Tenāli began, "I am punishing these pots. They are carrying dirty water of River Tungabhadra. If anyone falls sick, it would be due to this dirty water."

"Then you must throw away the dirty water. Why are you breaking the earthen pots? The water in the river is already dirty before it reached this point. Why are you causing losses to the poor fishermen? It's not their fault," the King explained.

"But, Your Majesty, did you not react like this when you punished the shopkeepers for selling powdered black pepper? You must punish the royal priest's brother, who supplies the powdered black pepper and not the innocent shopkeepers who were merely selling it."

This astonished the King who realised his folly and decided to release all the innocent shopkeepers the same day.

Life's Lesson

"The leader needs to be knowledgeable, fair and honest. He must have insights. A hasty decision without a thorough probe, does not become a good leader. He always need to identify the root cause, and then deal with it."

Wise Cracks

- Only the guilty should be punished.
- When the jury permits the guilty to escape, they augment the danger of the innocent.
- Justice is a great standing policy of civil society and the sum of all moral duty, so it should not be adulterated.
- The fundamentals of justice are that no one shall suffer wrong and that the public good be served.
- Injustice anywhere is a threat to justice everywhere. Let justice be done, though the heavens fall.

Quotable Nugget

"Only the actions of the just smell sweet and blossom in their just."

James Shirley

Testing Times

*A*fter two daughters, King Krishnadeva Rāya was blessed with a son. The jubilant King ordered celebrations throughout the Empire and invited everyone to the Royal Palace to bless the new born.

When Tenāli Raman arrived at the Palace, he looked at the baby boy and remarked, "Your Highness! This little boy will be even greater than his father." The King was very delighted. But when other courtiers saw this, they remarked, "O King! How can Tenāli be so sure that the Prince will be greater than you? How can he foretell something by just looking at your son? He is trying to flatter you. You ought to punish him."

The King knew that Tenāli was not the flattering kind, but he decided to find out what Tenāli had to say to defend himself. So he said, "Tenāli! Were you foretelling my son's future or were you trying to flatter me?"

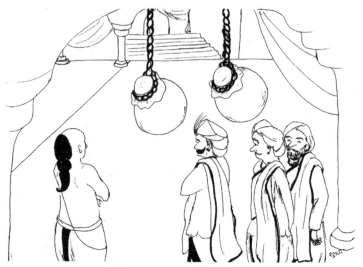

"Mission accomplished"

Tenāli replied, "O King! I have never flattered you. I could tell that your son would be greater than you by just observing him."

The King felt happy with Tenāli's response, but the envious courtiers said to the King, "If Tenāli claims to foretell things by just observing them, let's give him a test."

The King said, "I trust Tenāli and I know that he is very wise. But to prove to you that he is, I will give him a test. What do you propose I should do?"

Next day, the courtiers desired, "Please take two identical pots. Fill one with sand and leave the other one empty. Cover both of them with identical cloth and hang them from a ceiling. When Tenāli comes, ask him to tell which pot is empty and which one is full. He should do so only by observing the pots. He should not touch them."

The King agreed and ordered to do as suggested by the courtiers. Two identical pots — one filled with sand and the other one empty — with the mouth of both covered with identical cloth were hung up on the ceiling of the Palace with two ropes.

Then Tenāli was called. When Tenāli arrived, the King said, "Tenāli, I would like to find out if you could really foretell things by just observing them. I have a small test for you. You see the two pots hanging from the ceiling? One is filled with sand and the other one is empty. You have to tell which pot is full and which is empty without touching the pots. If you do that, I will know that you are not a flatterer."

Tenāli smiled. He understood the plan of the jealous courtiers to get rid of him. Then Tenāli walked close to the identical pots hanging from the ceiling. Everyone was keenly observing Tenāli and thinking what Tenāli is pondering in despair.

After a while, Tenāli looked at the King and said, "O King! The pot on my right is full of sand and the one on my left is empty."

The King said, "Tenāli, are you sure?"

Tenāli smiled and said, "I am as sure as I am that the newly born Prince will grow up to be greater than his father."

The King asked his guards to lower the pots and check. To everyone's surprise, they found that Tenāli was right. The pot on the left was empty while the pot on the right was full of sand.

The King cried out, "Tenāli! I am sorry that I listened to these jealous people, I should have trusted you. But please tell me how you were able to tell the difference. Even I was confused because the pots were so identical."

Tenāli smiled and said, "It was simple. All I did was just observe the pots carefully. Although they were tied by identical ropes, one pot was hanging a bit lower than the other. Obviously, the weight of the sand in the pot stretched the rope. I looked at the rope, the grooves of one were tight. But to make sure, I did something else. These fools thought that I was sighing in despair. In reality what I did was sigh near the pots, so that the wind that came out of my mouth blew into the pots. The one that was empty moved just a little bit, but the one that was full did not move at all."

The keen observation of Tenāli made everybody tightlipped. Their lips were sealed for the time being.

Life's Lesson

"There are many situations in life where we are reminded of the old wise saying 'there is no rule, that precludes the use of common sense.'"

Wise Cracks

- ☼ He alone is an alert observer, who can observe minutely without being observed. All men are born with two eyes, but with one tongue in order that they should see more and say less.
- ☼ It is the close observation of little things which is the secret of success.

Quotable Nugget

"Innocent and infinite are the pleasures of observation."

Henry James

Winner
All The Way

There was a wrestler named Atisura who lived in Srikalahasti. He conquered wrestlers of various courts and came to Vijayanagara with many badges. Atisura challenged the mightiest of the wrestlers of Vijayanagara. All the wrestlers in the Kingdom of King Rāya took alarm and were in a great fix.

Tenāli Raman saw all this and enquired from the unhappy wrestlers as to why they were so dejected? They exclaimed, "Up to this time, we have been living under King Rāya with great respect and dignity. Now time has come for us to lose our respect and our living also. A great wrestler has come to reduce us to this position. What shall we do?"

Tenāli said, "You please do not fear anything. Give me all your badges and follow me as if I'm your Chief."

"Formaidable challenger - poised for another battle"

Soon he decorated himself with all the badges, and assuming the name of Virakesari, took up his position with his followers in a tent opposite to that of Atisura. On seeing Virakesari garlanded with badges and followed by numerous wrestlers, Atisura thought within himself, 'This Chief seems to be my rival. Let me first of all ascertain his merit.'

So he sent a word to Virakesari that he had come to see him. But Virakesari sent back the following message, '. . . You need not come here now. You can make known your business in King Rāya's presence tomorrow in the Bhuvana Vijayam . . .' Atisura, on hearing this, was afraid at heart, thinking, 'What sort of wrestler he may be?'

Next day in the Bhuvana Vijayam, King Rāya permitted Atisura and Virakesari to wrestle in his presence. At that instance, Virakesari cautiously asked Atisura, "Is your method of wrestling the scientific method or the physical-force method?" After a deep thought, Atisura replied, "It is the scientific method."

Then Virakesari said, "I shall show some symbols of the scientific method of wrestling. If you explain what those symbols mean, I shall deem it proper to wrestle with you."

Atisura watchfully said, "Let it be so."

Thereupon, Virakesari joined together the middle fingers of Atisura's hands, and hit his own chest with them and then placed Atisura's two palms extended on his own shoulders, described a circle round his neck with the front finger, showed his right palm hanging upside down up to the hip, and waved his left fist. Atisura saw all these symbols, but could make nothing of them. He thought over all the symbols that he had learnt in wrestling, but in vain. Having waited for sometime, Virakesari snatched from him all the badges which he (Atisura) had acquired at other places and sounding his victorious drum, left the wrestling ring and entered his tent with his cheering followers behind him.

The next day King Rāya asked, "Tenāli! What is the meaning of all those symbols which you displayed yesterday as Virakesari?" Tenāli Raman, showing those symbols again, explained, "Atisura! If I approach you, you pierce me with your dagger in my chest and kill me. I shall then drop down stretched on the ground with my face upwards. Then who will protect my wife and child.

On hearing this, the King and the courtiers laughed heartily.

Life's Lesson

"Is it a dishonest ploy or an honest trick? Each one will have to answer, based on one's own perception. Is this area, black, white or shades of grey."

Wise Cracks

- ☼ The great need of life is not only knowledge, but a wise action at the right moment.
- ☼ An action is the presentation of thought.
- ☼ Suit the action to the word and the word to the action. With such balance one can conquer any calamity.
- ☼ Action makes more fortunes than caution.
- ☼ It is good to think well but it is divine to act well.
- ☼ The mere act of aiming at something big makes one big.

Quotable Nugget

"Out of action, action of any sort, there grows a peculiar, useful, everyday wisdom."

Frank Crane

A Special Encounter

$\mathcal{D}$uring King Krishnadeva Rāya's rule over Vijayanagara, the Mohammedan Sultans ruled the Delhi Sultanate. These Sultans were powerful and exercised supremacy over most of northern India. They intended to extend their dominance over whole of the Indian subcontinent and attempted to invade Hindu ruled states to grab them into their fold. For declaring war over Hindu ruled empires, the Sultans used to devise one or the other wicked ploy.

The Delhi Sultan once got a thought to offend the sentiments of King Rāya for which he sent a wedding invitation to the King through a personal messenger.

Going through the contents of the wedding invitation, the Bhuvana Vijayam and King Rāya were held speechless. The invitation read as:

"Sweet gestures"

Wedding Invitation

We propose to perform the marriage of the newly dug WELL in our Kingdom.

We take the pleasure of inviting all the wells of your kingdom to attend this auspicious ritual. Their (the wells') benign presence is solicited to shower blessings on our newly wedded WELL.

Place: Delhi

Date: XX/XX/XXXX   Sd/-

The Sultan of Delhi.

The tremor did not stop here. A warning letter was attached to the invitation which read that in case the King failed to send all the wells of his empire to Delhi for the ceremony, it would be treated as an offence and the King along with his subjects will be liable to face the fury of the Delhi Sultan.

King Rāya on receiving the invitation and the warning letter could not understand what to do about the invitation. Everyone knew that sending wells from one place to another is practically impossible. The King in total confusion took advice of his courtiers and the ashtadiggajas, but the invitation being strange and weird, no one was able to suggest any amicable solution that could be effective in avoiding any rift between the two Kingdoms.

At last, the King sought the help of Tenāli Raman. When the whole sequence was narrated to Tenāli, he told the King, "Sir! The Delhi Sultan is attempting to humiliate the Hindu rituals and customs. You know Hindus have a ritual of performing enlivening (Prathistha) to the newly dug wells. A wonderful thought must have struck the Sultan's mind to perform marriage of the well instead of prathistha to the well." Tenāli continued, "There is no problem either with the invitation or the warning letter. There is nothing to worry. I will attempt an amicable solution in Bhuvana Vijayam tomorrow."

The next day, in the tensed Bhuvana Vijayam where everyone was worried about the solution to the Delhi Sultan created problem, Tenāli Raman stood from his seat and started reading a reply that he had prepared by him on behalf of King Rāya :

"To His Excellency, the Sultan of Delhi . . .

We acknowledge your invitation inviting our wells for the wedding of a WELL in your kingdom. We are glad and grateful that you remembered us on this auspicious occasion. On receiving your invitation, we immediately read the message to all the wells of our Kingdom. Those wells are resenting your wells, as they did not attend their (wells in Vijayanagara Empire) wedding ceremonies.

Hence, we keep you informed that if your wells personally come to the Vijayanagara and invite, our wells will definitely oblige the invitation. Therefore, you are requested to send your wells here to invite our wells personally to the wedding ritual. Once your wells come here, our wells and we together will come to Delhi for the wedding.

Hoping to see your wells at the earliest,

Place: Vijayanagara (Hampi)

Date: XX/XX/XXXX

Yours' sincerely,

Sri Krishnadeva Rāya,

"Vijayanagara Ruler"

The entire Bhuvana Vijayam cheered at once on hearing the reply intellectually composed by Tenāli and appreciated.

This reply was sent to Delhi Sultan through a personal messenger. The Sultan of Delhi was taken aback with the reply received and questioned the messenger, "How can we send the wells with you?"

Receiving no reply from the messenger, without any second thought the Sultan dropped the proposals of humiliating the Hindu rituals along with the thought of waging wars unnecessarily against the Hindu ruled Kingdoms.

Life's Lesson

"What is the difference between being 'cunning and being 'smart'?

Sometimes it is necessary to be cunning, in order to get the better of an opponent who is being unreasonable."

Wise Cracks

- ☼ Vanity makes men ridiculous, pride makes them horrible and ambition terrible.
- ☼ Men with vanity herald insults on others.
- ☼ An injury is much sooner forgotten than an insult.
- ☼ If you utter insults, you will also hear them.
- ☼ It is bad enough to be bad, but to be bad in bad taste is unpardonable.

Quotable Nugget

"The belief in a supernatural source of evil is not necessary; men alone are quite capable of every wickedness."

Joseph Conrad

Prize Catch

King Krishnadeva Rāya used to personally undertake regular tours of his vast empire to hear the grievances of people and tried to redress them then and there itself.

Once the King accompanied by Tenāli Raman was riding through the countryside of his newly conquered territory: Srirangapatnam. He met a peasant there.

Ever concerned about the welfare of his subjects, the King asked Tenāli Raman to enquire about the earnings of the peasant and the ways he spend his earnings. Tenāli approached the peasant to enquire. After a detailed discussion with the peasant, Tenāli returned to the King to give him the report.

"My Lord, the peasant has one mar (plot of 16 to 18 acres) and is a regular payer of land revenue to the state based on the yield. The peasant earns forty varahas each month and supports a large family, Your Majesty," replied Tenāli.

"Money matters"

174

"And how does the peasant spends his forty varahas?" the King continued to ask.

"Ten on himself, ten he gives in gratitude, ten he gives back and ten he gives on interest," replied Tenāli.

The King was left confused to hear this and asked Tenāli to explain.

"A part of the money he spends on himself," said Tenāli, "a part on his wife in gratitude for all she does for the house; a part on his aged parents to pay them back for all that they did for the peasant and a part on his children. He expects the children will pay him back with interest by looking after him and his wife in their old age," Tenāli continued to explain.

"You have provided me a fine riddle, Tenāli," said the King excitedly, "Tenāli, please keep the answer a secret for sometime, at least till you've seen my face a hundred times."

"I surely will," assured Tenāli.

That very evening, the King put the same brainteaser to the ashtadiggajas in the Bhuvana Vijayam. The King told them how the peasant spends his earnings and asked them to explain what the peasant had meant by saying, 'he spends ten varahas on himself, ten he gives in gratitude, ten he gives back and ten he gives on interest'."

The ashtadiggajas did not know the answer but Allasani Peddana one of them assured to have a reply to the puzzle within a day.

Allasani Peddana knew of Tenāli accompanying the King during his meeting with the peasant. Peddana approached Tenāli and asked him the answer to the riddle. Tenāli, at first, refused to tell but was eventually persuaded to do so by Peddana in return of a gift of a bag of varahas (gold coins). When Peddana returned to the Royal Palace and told the King the answer to the riddle, the monarch guessed that Tenāli had broken his promise of silence.

The King sent for Tenāli and asked him why he had betrayed his trust.

"Tenāli, didn't I tell you not to reveal the answer till you had seen my face a hundred times?" demanded the King angrily.

"Sir, I have kept my promise. I did see your face a hundred times before I told Peddana the answer, Your Majesty," replied Tenāli, "Peddana gave me a bag of hundred varahas and each of the varaha had your face on it."

The King was delighted with Tenāli's wit and rewarded him handsomely.

LIFE'S LESSON

"Many actions are taken based on what we will benefit more from. Should you follow the letter of the law(promise) or the spirit of the law(promise)? Each one of us has to work this out with his own conscience."

Wise Cracks

- ☼ Do not wait for extraordinary circumstances to do good, try to use opportunities available in everyday situations.
- ☼ To be a great man, it is necessary to account and use all the opportunities.
- ☼ Opportunities are rare but a wise man will make more opportunities than he finds.
- ☼ No great man ever complains of want of opportunities. An optimist sees an opportunity in every calamity; a pessimist sees calamity in every opportunity.

Quotable Nugget

"Opportunity has hair in front, behind she is bald. If you seize her by the forelock, you may hold her, but if suffered to escape, not Jupiter himself can catch her again."

From the Latin

Lost
and Found

Once a beggar found a leather purse that someone had dropped in the busy marketplace of Hampi. Opening the purse, the beggar discovered that it contained 100 varahas (gold coins). At that moment, the beggar heard a merchant shouting, "A reward! A reward to the one who finds my leather purse!"

Being a truthful man, the beggar came forward and handed the purse to the merchant saying, "Here is your purse, Sir. May I now have my reward?"

"Reward?" mocked the merchant, greedily counting his varahas, "Why should I reward you? The purse I dropped had 200 varahas in it. You've already stolen more than the reward! Go away or I'll tell the royal guards."

"I'm an honest man," said the beggar daringly, "let us take this matter to the Royal Court to have justice."

Caught lacking

Both went to the Bhuvana Vijayam, the Royal Court and narrated the entire episode to the King and the ashtadiggajas. The King patiently listened to both the sides about the episode and asked his bright ashtadiggaja, Tenāli Raman to settle the case amicably.

After giving a brief thought, Tenāli said, "I believe you both. Justice is possible! Merchant, you stated that the leather purse you had lost contained 200 varahas. Well, that's a considerable cost. But the purse this beggar found had only 100 varahas. Therefore, it couldn't be the one you lost."

And, with that, the King upheld Tenāli's verdict and gave the purse and all the varahas it contained to the beggar.

Life's Lesson

"Inspite of what many people may say, staying with the truth has its own rewards. Those who bend the truth, are invariably found out. Some sooner, many later. There is always a step between the cup and the lip; for the person who is dishonest."

Wise Cracks

☼ Honesty is an attitude of accepting reality as it is.

☼ Lies will get any man into trouble, but honesty is its own defence. Do not consider anything for your personal interest that makes you break your word, quit your modesty, or incline you to any practice which will not bear the light, or look the world in the face.

Quotable Nugget

"Though it is a bit difficult, but it is always better to be sincere and honest."

Anonymous

Left High and Dry

King Krishnadeva Rāya had some superior quality saplingless brinjal (aubergine) plants growing in his private garden. No one was allowed to view the garden without the King's permission. The King alone tasted the saplingless brinjal.

Once King Rāya invited his royal courtiers to a feast in which saplingless brinjal vegetable was served. Tenāli Raman enjoyed the vegetable so much that he discussed about it with his wife on returning home. On hearing Tenāli's comments, his wife insisted on tasting the royal saplingless brinjal.

"How can I get them for you?" Tenāli asked his wife, "King Rāya is so possessive about the vegetable that he can detect the theft of even a single brinjal from his garden. And, I'm sure that he would get the thief's head chopped off if he was caught red-handed stealing the brinjal."

"Strategic time out"

But Tenāli's wife begged him to allow her to taste the brinjal. Tenāli was helpless. After much discussion, he agreed to his wife's persistent demand.

Next night, he silently jumped into the Royal Garden and plucked a few succulent brinjals. His wife cooked them with fervour and was all praise for the taste. She wanted to let their six-year-old son also taste the vegetable, but Tenāli asked her not to do so.

"Don't make such a mistake," Tenāli warned her, "if he happens to tell somebody, we will be in deep trouble." But his wife did not agree and insisted, "How is that possible? How can we eat something whose taste we shall remember forever and not share it with our beloved son! Please find a way out, so that he gets to taste the vegetable and nobody is able to prove that we stole it from the Royal Garden."

Tenāli Raman had no option but to nod his head in agreement to his wife's suggestion. However, before making his son taste the vegetable, Tenāli filled a bucket full of water and went upstairs to the roof where his son was sleeping. He poured the water all over the child. Then he picked up the child and said, "It is raining heavily. Let us go inside the house and sleep."

Once inside the house, Tenāli got the child's clothes changed and gave him the vegetable to eat. Tenāli again remarked loudly that as it was raining heavily outside, the little boy should sleep in the room.

The next day King Rāya came to know of the theft in his garden. The royal gardener who kept a head count of each vegetable and flower, found four fleshy brinjals missing. It became the talk of the town. King Rāya declared a huge prize on the thief's head.

The Dandanayaka (Royal Commander) suspected that only Tenāli was capable of such a bold act. He let the King know about his suspicion. The King said, "I know Tenāli is very clever and always gets out of the charges on one pretext or the other. It is better that we call his son. We will find the truth from his son only. Tenāli will lie to get out of any situation, but he would never ask his child to do so."

Tenāli Raman's son was called to the Bhuvana Vijayam. He was asked which vegetable he ate the night before. The child replied, "Brinjal and it was the tastiest vegetable I've ever eaten." The Dandanayaka told Tenāli, "Now you will have to accept your guilt Raman."

"Why should I when I'm not guilty?" replied Tenāli, "Last night, the boy went to sleep very early and seems to have had many dreams. That is why he is talking nonsense about brinjals and heavy rain and what not. Ask him if it rained last night or not."

Accordingly, the Dandanayaka asked the child, "How was the weather last night? Was the sky clear or did it rain?" The child innocently replied, "It rained heavily last night. All my clothes got wet when I slept on the roof. Thereafter, I had to sleep indoors." The fact was that not even a single drop of rain had fallen on Vijayanagar that day.

The King and the Dandanayaka had no option but to get rid of their suspicions in the face of such apparent madness. They apologised to Tenāli Raman for having suspected him.

LIFE'S LESSON

"Should one be pressurised by the spouse into doing wrong and even committing theft? Is it right to accede to such request or even commands? Is it worldly right to use your superior mental capabilities to wriggle out of the situation and escape unscathed? Does this do justice to the divine that has blessed you with such abilities? These are questions we have to ask ourselves."

Wise Cracks

- Strategic Planning forms a basis for action orientation in our day-to-day life.
- Planning comprises of analysis of current situation, anticipating the future, setting objectives and deciding the activities to engage for achievement of pre-determined goals.
- Efficient individuals develop capabilities to get extraordinary results from ordinary situations just by strategic planning.

Quotable Nugget

"When schemes are laid in advance, it is surprising how often the circumstances fit in with them."

Sir William Ocler

Meeting of Minds

*T*hathacharya, the Rajaguru (the royal teacher-cum-priest) was always devising nasty ways to insult Tenāli Raman in front of King Krishnadeva Rāya and the Bhuvana Vijayam.

One day while the King and his courtiers were just about to deliberate on issues regarding Kingdom's governance, Tenāli came upon Thathacharya who excitedly said, "Tenāli Raman, do you know what I have just heard about one of your disciples?"

"Rajaguru, I beg to wait a moment please," Tenāli replied. "Before you tell me anything, I'd just like you to reply to few of my simple questions."

"Time for soul searching"

The King and the courtiers eagerly turned their attention towards the ensuing witty battle of the two scholars.

"Answers to Questions . . . What's that?" exclaimed Thathacharya hurriedly.

"That's right," Tenāli continued. "Before you talk to me about any of my disciples or any such trivial issue, let's take a moment to test what you're going to say and its relevance. This momentarily question and answer session will definitely save everybody's precious time discussing trivial issues. The first question which I intend to ask you is the 'Truth Inquest'. Have you made absolutely sure that what you are about to tell me is true, real and factual?"

"Oh no!" Thathacharya said, "actually I have just heard about it."

"All right," said Tenāli, "so you don't really know if it's true or not. It may be a gossip, a rumour or simply a grapevine. Now let's try the second question, the 'Goodness Inquest'. Is what you are about to tell me about my disciples something good and virtuous?"

"No, on the contrary..." said Thathacharya.

"So," Tenāli interrupted, "you want to tell me something bad and awful about my disciples, even though you're not certain whether it's true or not?"

Thathacharya shrugged, a little embarrassed.

Tenāli continued, "You may still succeed, because there is a third question - the 'Usefulness Inquest'. Is what you want to tell me about my disciples going to be useful and constructive to me?"

"Well it....no, not really..." remarked Thathacharya.

"Well," concluded Tenāli, "if what you want to tell me is neither true nor good nor even useful, then why tell it to me at all and waste my and everybody's time and energy?"

Thathacharya felt defeated and ashamed in front of the King and the courtiers.

Life's Lesson

"If we use the truth, good, useful(TGU) index in all inward and outward communication, we will save time and also lead more constructive lives. The TGU index will help to discipline us in both our social life and in our professional life."

> ## Wise Cracks
> ☼ Make haste in doing good, useful and truthful deeds; check your mind from evil because the mind of the person who is slow in doing meritorious actions delights in evil.
>
> ☼ Virtue is not to be considered in the light of mere innocence, or abstaining from doing harm; but as the exertion of our faculties in doing good and truthful acts.

Quotable Nugget

A swarm of Bees Worth Living--

B-patient, B-prayerful, B-humble, B-mild,

B-wise, as a Solomon, B-meek as a child;

B-studious, B-thoughtful, B-loving, B-kind;

B-sure you make matter subservient to mind;

B-cautious, B-prudent, B-trustful, B-true,

B-courteous to all, B-friendly with few;

B-temperate in argument, pleasure and wine,

B-careful of conduct, of money, and time.

Anonymous

✺✺✺

Intelligent Strikes

Tenāli Raman had a garden in his house where flowers and vegetables grew in abundance. The garden had a deep well at one corner.

One late evening, while strolling the terrace after having dinner, Tenāli observed the plants in his garden withering due to summer heat and lack of proper watering. When he carefully observed the plants, he noticed some movement in the dense bushes in his garden. Soon he realised some thieves to be hiding there.

Pretending to be unaware of the thieves' presence, Tenāli screamed out to his wife that due to increased number of robberies taking place in the city

"Something for everyone"

everyday, she should be more careful with her jewellery and valuables. Tenāli loudly suggested her wife that as a precautionary measure they should hide their valuables in a big iron trunk and throw it into their garden well. In this way, all their valuables will be safe.

Suggesting all this, Tenāli quietly entered inside, and informed his wife about some thieves hiding in the garden. Tenāli explained to his wife that the thieves usually frequent their house and thus, they should be taught a tough lesson this time.

Tenāli explained to his wife that in order to deceive the thieves, they should secretly place heavy stones inside an iron trunk instead of jewellery or valuables and throw it into the garden well. In this manner, they will pretend to be hiding their valuables in an iron trunk thrown in the well and thus mislead the thieves.

Soon the thieve, who were secretly hiding in the undergrowth saw Tenāli and his wife painstakingly dragging the iron trunk from within their house and throw the weighty trunk into the well. The two, then, declared aloud that they are going to sleep and went inside bolting all doors and windows.

A little later, all the four thieves came in action. With a view to flee with the valuables, the thieves tried to pull out the heavy trunk from the well with full might, but the trunk was too heavy and could not be dragged out of the well.

Failing to pull the trunk from the well, one of the thieves suggested drawing all the water from the well first, and then dragging the trunk out of the well. Accordingly, the thieves began their laborious job of drawing water from the well.

The thieves carried the job of emptying the well till daybreak. Once sufficient water was drawn from the well, they went deep down the well and, some how, managed to drag out the heavy trunk. When they broke open the lock of the trunk, to their utter astonishment they found heavy stones in the trunk. Tenāli secretly saw the entire episode from inside and arrived in the garden smilingly.

The thieves seeing Tenāli entering the garden tried to make their way out. Perceiving the thieves to be fleeing, Tenāli exclaimed, "My dear friends, no need to fear from me. I am not going to catch you. Rather I am thankful to you because you have very laboriously watered all my withering plants.

The thieves realised that they have been cleverly trapped by Tenāli and pleaded forgiveness from Tenāli.

Life's Lesson

"The accepted definition of a true leader is - one who can get people to do what he wants done, and stops from interfering while they are doing it. In that sense Tenali was not only a wit and wise but also a leader."

Wise Cracks

- ☼ Just as our eyes need light in order to see, our minds need ideas in order to conceive.
- ☼ Nothing is more compelling than an idea whose time has come.
- ☼ He who wishes to fulfil his mission in the world must be a man of good ideas.
- ☼ The idea is the philosophy which forms the basis of all actions.

Quotable Nugget

"A man may die, nations may rise and fall, but an idea lives on. Ideas have endurance without death."

J.F. Kennedy

Yours is Here

One day in the Bhuvana Vijayam, Tenāli Raman appeared to be very unhappy. King Krishnadeva Rāya noticed this and enquired, "Tenāli! Why are you so remorseful today? What do you want?"

Tenāli replied in a murky tone, "Yes, Your Honour! Today, I am really upset. The astrologers have told me that I shall die within two months but I am not at all thinking about my life now. I am only grieving that after I am gone, there will be none to protect my family as I have been protecting it. I am worried for my family."

Hearing Tenāli, King Rāya clarified, "Tenāli! Do not worry at all. You have always been loyal to me and had always endeavoured to save my prestige. I shall protect your entire family ten times more carefully and diligently than you have been doing. This is not at all a great affair for me." Thus, the King consoled Tenāli Raman and tried to pacify him.

"Missing in action"

Thereafter, Tenāli pretended to be sick to everybody and get worse day by day. At last, Tenāli plotted to spread a rumour that he was no more. While doing so, he secured all his money, jewels and precious vessels in a large trunk, and also hid himself into that trunk.

As soon as King Rāya heard that his witty jester and the ashtadiggaja Tenāli had died, he sent a troop of royal soldiers and ordered them to bring away at once the jester's large money box, expecting to find in it large wealth. The royal soldiers accordingly obeyed the orders and brought the big trunk to the Royal Palace.

The moment the trunk came, King Rāya with great interest and curiosity opened the trunk and looked in. On seeing Tenāli in the trunk, he shockingly yelled, "What is this?! Tenāli, everybody told that you were dead."

Tenāli without any argument reacted, "O My Highness! How can I die confiding in you? Are you the person who will protect my family attentively after my death?"

The King was ashamed to listen to Tenāli's remarks but remained silent.

Life's Lesson

"Trust is not a one-time development. Trust has to be put to test, over and over again. Many people make instant commitments and you trust that they will fulfil theim. But like cutting knives which have to be sharpened again and again, trust has to be renewed regularly and never taken for granted."

Wise Cracks

- ☼ Hypocrisy (double-standards) is folly and is the only vice which can't be forgiven.
- ☼ It is easier, safer and natural to be the thing which a man aims to appear, than to keep up the appearance of what he is not.
- ☼ A man is at his worst when he pretends to be good.
- ☼ The repentance of a hypocrite is itself hypocrisy.

Quotable Nugget

"False face must hide what the false heart doth know."

William Shakespeare

Who's Who

"*T*ell me Tenāli! Of the four varnas (catagories) of our society, which catagory has usually more intelligent and sharp mind and which has simple and straightforward people?" once King Krishnadeva Rāya enquired from Tenāli Raman.

"Your Honour, the businessmen (vaishya) as a class are more intelligent and clever. On the other hand, the Brahmins are generally simple and somber," Tenāli Raman at once responded.

Opposing Tenāli's statement, the King said, "How can you say so Tenāli? Brahmins are supposed to be more scholarly and hence cleverer. Businessmen are generally uneducated and unqualified and hence not very wise!"

"Discovering a ritual beyond rituals"

Tenāli Raman said, "No, Your Majesty. I can prove the genuineness of my opinion provided you don't interfere."

The King agreed to Tenāli's suggestion.

A week later, Tenāli went to Thathacharya(Rajaguru) and said respectfully, "O Rajaguru, the King has desired for your tuft of hair on head (known as choti, the hair at the crown left unshaven even when tonsure ceremony is performed among the orthodox Hindus). Are you prepared to have it shaved?"

The Rajaguru was noticeably disturbed. How could the Rajaguru get his the turt of hair on his head shaved off? it is evidently the symbol of his religious faith and devotion. The Rajaguru was very proud of his prominent, long and heavy tuft and was not prepared to have it shaved. He said, "Well Tenāli Raman, I have maintained my tuft with great efforts. How can I have it shaved?"

"You can get any price you want for it," Tenāli Raman offered.

Now the Rajaguru was in a fix. He never wanted his it happen, but at the same time the lure of money was difficult to resist. He also wanted to pretend that he gave great worth to religion. At last he said, "Since it is a royal order, I will have it shaved, even though I don't want to do it. As I cannot defy the royal order, it will be followed. But you will have to give me ten varahas (gold coins) in return."

"No problem. You will get them soon!" said Tenāli Raman.

And against ten varahas, the Rajaguru allowed the barber to shave off his well-nurtured and well-oiled tuft of head at the centre of the skull.

Next Tenāli Raman sent for the leading businessman of Vijayanagara named Sukumara. He too had a prominent choti.

Tenāli Raman said to him, "The King needs your choti for some reason. Are you prepared to get it shaved off?"

Sukumara replied, "Everything of the empire is our King's property, including our lives. The King may take it whenever he wants it. But please remember one thing that I'm a poor man."

"Don't worry," assured Tenāli Raman, "you will get the price you demand for your choti."

"That's very kind of you, but...." Sukumara said hesitatingly.

Tenāli Raman was annoyed and asked, "But what...?"

"Actually the issue is very sensitive," began the businessman watchfully, "it was only for this choti that I had to spend ten thousand varahas in my daughter's marriage. You know my choti symbolises my prestige. Last year when my father died, I had to spend another five thousand varahas in his funeral ceremony for the sake of this choti only. My choti is quiet precious," concluded Sukumara while lovingly stroking his choti.

"It means for this choti you had spent fifteen thousand varahas. All right, you will have fifteen thousand varahas from the royal treasury and let the barber chop it off," affirmed Tenāli Raman.

When fifteen thousand varahas were paid to Sukumara, the barber was called in, who began to wet Sukumara's choti for shaving off. As soon as the barber took out his razor, Sukumara said in an authoritative tone, "Be careful, you barber! You know this choti is now the King's property. Consider it as if you are shaving off the choti of the mighty King Krishnadeva Rāya!"

The King was sitting near and watching this ceremony. Hearing Sukumara's remarks, he lost his temper. It appeared absolute insulting to the King to hear someone referring to the shaving of the King's choti. The King roared, "Take this ill-mannered person away from my sight. Throw out this disrespectful businessman."

And Sukumara was brutally thrown out, but he didn't mind as he was richer by fifteen thousand varahas.

Later Tenāli Raman told the King, "Your Honour, didn't you see the shrewdness of that businessman. He not only received fifteen thousand varahas but also managed to keep his choti intact, whereas our Rajaguru, the leading Brahmin allowed his choti to be shaved off for just ten varahas!"

The King had nothing but to admit Tenāli's contention about the cleverness of the people belonging to business class, and the simple nature of Brahmins.

Life's Lesson

"People will accept your pronouncements if they are supported by experiential proof, this creates credibility. If the pronouncements are not substantiated, these remain only opinions or even worse, suppositions. The more credibility you have, the greater the trust of these around you."

Wise Cracks

- ☼ Facts do not cease to exist even when they are ignored.
- ☼ Digging up facts may be a hard job, but it is much better than jumping at conclusions.
- ☼ Facts do not change; it is only our opinions which change.
- ☼ It is better to say that our opinions depend upon our lives and habits, than to say that our lives and habits depend on our opinions.
- ☼ It takes ages to destroy a popular opinion.

Quotable Nugget

"Remember that all things are only opinion and that it is in your power to think as you please."

Marcus Aurelius

There It Goes, Again

*T*he 'Fool of the Year' was an annual event organised with enthusiasm in the Bhuvana Vijayam (The Royal Court). The 'Fool of the Year' competition was open to all the courtiers of King Krishnadeva Rāya. All the people keenly looked forward to the event as the winner stood to gain a handsome prize of 5,000 varahas (gold coins). The trouble was that Tenāli Raman always won the contest.

One year, all the courtiers decided that Tenāli must be kept out of the contest. So, the courtiers bribed Tenāli's servant with a hefty sum to lock him in his room to prevent Tenāli from reaching the Royal Palace in time for the event.

Things happened as planned and Tenāli was prevented from reaching the Royal Palace in time to take part in the contest. Consequently, Tenāli reached

"A new challenge every day"

the Royal Palace after the contest was already over. Just as the name of the winner for the contest was about to be announced, seeing Tenāli entering the Palace, King Rāya asked him the reason for not reaching the Royal Palace in time and participate in the event.

Citing the reason, Tenāli told King Rāya that he was in an urgent need of 100 varahas and thus had been engaged in trying to raise the said amount.

"If you had participated in the contest, you might have won the prize money and your problem would have been solved," said the King, "you've behaved very foolishly," continued the King with a chuckle.

"I am really a fool, Sir," said Tenāli pitifully.

"Tenāli! Today you have acted in a very strange manner. You're not just a fool, but you're the greatest fool I've ever seen!" exclaimed King Rāya.

"That means I have won the contest, Sir!" said Tenāli excitedly.

King Rāya realised that he had made a slip but was very proud to acknowledge it and to the embarrassment of the other courtiers again declared Tenāli Raman as the winner of 'Fool of the Year' contest by decorating the witty jester with the handsome prize money.

LIFE'S LESSON

"It is the ability of a WINNER to turn a disadvantage into an advantage. To turn a negative into a positive. To light a candle, instead of cursing the darkness."

Wise Cracks

- ☼ Often, while calling others fool, we are perhaps making a fool of ourselves.
- ☼ Wise men have more to learn from fools than fools from wise men. For one word or action, a man is often deemed to be wise or foolish.
- ☼ We should be careful indeed what we say or what we do.

Quotable Nugget

"Every man is a fool in some man's opinion."

Spanish Proverb

The Namesake

One winter afternoon, while returning from the royal palace, Tenāli Raman came across a beggar. Immediately Tenāli took out a silver coin from his pocket to offer it to the beggar as donation. The beggar refused to accept the donation being made by Tenāli and said, "Sir, I don't need any donations. I know you are the clever ashtadiggaja of the royal court. I just want a suggestion to my problem which is disturbing me since long."

"Ohhhh . . . Tell me what is your problem," Tenāli asked passionately.

The beggar hesitatingly said, "No doubt I am an unfortunate beggar, but I have a strong desire that the people should call me 'sethji'. Unluckily, I am unable to find a solution to this."

Tenāli paused for a while and then said, "I can solve your problem. Very soon, you will be called 'sethji' by everyone. You just have to do what I advice .

"The name says it all"

. .you stand a little far from this point and when someone calls you 'sethji-sethji', just run after him pretending to beat him," Tenāli continued to explain.

The beggar did as advised by Tenāli and stood at a distance. Meanwhile, Tenāli caught hold of a few mischievous boys playing nearby and pointing towards the beggar told to the boys, "Can you see that person standing alone? That person feels very irritated when anyone calls him 'sethji'!"

This remark of Tenāli was sufficient for the playful boys for another mischief. Soon all boys assembled close to the beggar and started teasing by calling him 'sethji-sethji'. The beggar ran after the boys pretending to hurt them. This pleased the naughty boys more who repeatedly teased him by calling 'sethji-sethji'. Other people on noticing this also started making mockery of the beggar by calling 'sethji'. The more the beggar ran after the people, the more the people teased him. This went for days and soon the beggar was famous as 'sethji' throughout Hampi.

Life's Lesson

"Often, even the most ridiculous requests can be met, if you put on a thinking hat and indulge in 'lateral' thinking. But we need to determine whether to spend our time on ridiculous request in the first place."

Wise Cracks

☼ It is a matter of simplest demonstration that the more the fire is covered up, the more it burns.

☼ Suppression enhances the effect of an act manifold.

☼ The noose (ring) across the nose of the horse, the walls of the dam restricting the river water, the crown (cork) of the soda water bottle etc., boost the hidden power lying within by restricting them.

☼ The hidden power should be used to our advantage for achieving our goals.

Quotable Nugget

"Man's natural instinct is never toward what is sound and true; it is toward what is suspicious and false."

H.L. Mencken

A Tactful Move

$\mathcal{A}$ssociation of Vijayanagara Empire with European Empires greatly developed during King Krishnadeva Rāya regime. Many European travellers such as Domingo Paes, Fernao Nuniz and Niccolo Da Conti visited Vijayanagara to view its magestic appearance during that period. These travellers spent noteworthy time at Bhuvana Vijayam(Royal Court) and even gave crucial account of their visits.

Once, the well-off wife of the Mayor of a European County(province) was attracted by King Krishnadeva Rāya's fame, She was lured by the tales of the intellectual depth of the ashtadiggajas and scholars of Bhuvana Vijayam. The lady wished to visit the Royal Court accompanied by the European traveller

"Leaving an impression"

Fernao Nuniz. She came to Vijayanagara. She had heard that the speech of the King and his courtiers' was full of learning and wisdom and that they used to teach valuable lessons through proverbs and anecdotes. She was curious to know if what she had heard was true. She had also heard of the King and his courtiers' uncanny ability to solve the most difficult puzzles, which she meant to test.

The King greeted the lady to the Bhuvana Vijayam. In order to test the King and his courtiers, the lady held two beautiful garlands of flowers, one in her right hand and one in her left. The flowers in one hand were real and those in the other artificial. "O King, which is the true garland," she asked, "and which is the false one?"

The King was still. The ashtadiggajas and the courtiers doubted whether the King or any of them would be able to solve the riddle. The King kept gazing at the garlands in clear confusion. "Which is the true garland?" the lady asked again.

The wise ashtadiggajas and the scholars stood soundless. Tenāli Raman too gaped speechless.

While Tenāli Raman was pondering for the answer, he noticed a swarm of bees bustling about a withered rose flower just outside the window. "Open the window. Let gentle breeze flow in," Tenāli said eagerly. As soon as the window was opened, the bees flew in and settled on the flowers in the lady's right hand. It was clear that the garland in her right hand was the true one.

Seeing this, the lady stood impressed with the wit of the King's courtiers. She praised the king and the courtiers sweetly.

LIFE'S LESSON

"A hundred people might have seen the bee. Only one person knew how to make capital of the situation. Why is this? Because it needs a prepared mind to be confronted with opportunity. This is true of Tenali Raman, Louis Pasteur and Alexander Fleming to all others without a 'prepared mind' these are opportunities which can be passed by.

Wise Cracks

- ☼ A hair perhaps divides the false and true.
- ☼ Sometimes it is easier to see clearly into the liar than into the man who tells the truth.
- ☼ While truth stands the test of time, lies are soon exposed.
- ☼ Language of truth is unadorned and always simple. What is required is sheer presence of mind and common sense for distinguishing truth from falsehood.
- ☼ Truth is truth, whether it is believed or not.

Quotable Nugget

"Craft must have clothes, but truth loves to go naked."

Thomas Fuller

Bare in
Mind

One day, King Krishnadeva Rāya overslept till even late after sunrise. When the barber came for shaving the King, he found the King asleep. He shaved and trimmed the hair of the King so watchfully that the King continued to sleep without any disturbance. The barber after completing his task left the place in all silence.

King Rāya on waking up saw the mirror, and found himself to be neatly shaved and the hair nicely cut. He much delighted at the expertise of the barber. He sent for the barber and asked him what he wanted.

"My Honour!" the barber said shyly, "you have been very grateful to me. My only unfulfilled wish is to become a Brahmin. Kindly make my wish fulfilled."

"Speed, skill, agression"

Hearing the wish of the barber, the King immediately sent for several Brahmins and said to them, "This barber is to be converted into a Brahmin within two months. My orders are to be obeyed firmly failing which stern action would be taken against all of you and all the privileges bestowed upon you will be withdrawn." The Brahmins felt upset at unwise instructions of the King. But to obey the King's stern orders, the Brahmins took away the barber.

The news of barber turning into a Brahmin spread in the city and the entire Brahmin community thought the King's decision of transforming the barber into a Brahmin to be totally unrealistic. The Brahmin community further thought that such an act of transformation might give way for many others to long for the wish which is against Dharma. Distressed, they went to Tenāli Raman for help who assured the Brahmins to find a solution soon.

Obeying the royal orders, everyday the Brahmins took the barber along the sacred banks of Tungabhadra-Krishna River doab and made him bathe twice daily. The Brahmins taught him to perform divine rituals and pronounce sanctified chants and holy prayers and many other such things.

While the process of converting the barber into a Brahmin was being carried out with full fervour; one day the King went to the River doab to ascertain the progress. There he found the Brahmins teaching the barber to recite hymns and perform rites.

At the same time, a little far from this place, the King observed that Tenāli was standing by the side of a black dog and chanting something or the other. Tenāli was performing certain rites and bathing the dog with the river water by scrubbing it hard. While the Brahmins and the barber continued chanting the hymns, King Rāya slowly walked close to Tenāli and asked, "Tenāli! What are you doing to this dog?" Tenāli very courteously replied, "I am transforming this black dog into a white cow."

The King laughed mockingly at Tenāli's statement and said, "Tenāli . . . how can this black dog, perhaps, any dog turn into a white cow if you chant some hymns and give it a dip in the holy river?"

Innocently Raman said, "Kindly forgive me for my stupidity. But, why can't this black dog be turned into a white cow, when a barber is being transformed into a Brahmin?"

King Rāya stopped laughing and started thinking. He understood that Tenāli was doing this with a purpose to open his eyes. Immediately he called the barber and told him, "It is not possible to turn you into a Brahmin. forget this desire and ask for another one."

The barber obediently said, "My Lord! I am happy with your kindness, I do not need anything," and left for home. King Rāya felicitated Tenāli for opening his eyes and protecting from doing things against the Dharma.

Life's Lesson

"Any transformation may be difficult but it should be feasible and desirable. Change and transformations brought about by fiat are not only indesirable but will not last long."

Wise Cracks

- ☼ Personal qualities and virtues are healthy and good for the soul.
- ☼ They are developed gradually with persistence and patience.
- ☼ There is no shortcut route or ready way to acquire good qualities and virtues.
- ☼ All bow to virtues and good qualities but you cannot legislate for them.

Quotable Nugget

"Virtue is better than immortality and life kingdoms, sons, glory, wealth, all these do not equal one sixteenth part of the value of virtue."

Mahabharata

Battle of Wits

*T*hathacharya, the Rajaguru always tried to get the better of Tenāli Raman. One fine morning Thathacharya noticed a succulent and ripe apple growing on a tree in his garden. He knocked it down, wrapped it in a muslin cloth and waited for Tenāli Raman to come by.

When Tenāli did come, Thathacharya called out to Tenāli, "I have a riddle for you to solve," he said, "can you tell me what fruit is wrapped in this cloth? If you guess correctly, you may take any one thing from my house that you can carry out with your two hands; if you fail I'll come to your house and carry away something."

"Here to the rescue"

"All right," said Tenāli Raman, always ready to match his wits with Thathacharya.

"It must be a guava," replied Tenāli meekly.

"No," said Thathacharya smiling, "I'll give you two more guesses," continued Thathacharya.

"It is the season for pomegranate, so it must be a pomegranate." explained Tenāli.

"No! It's not a pomegranate. Now it's your last guess," said Thathacharya.

"Then, it's an orange?" said Tenāli humbly.

"You've failed grossly Tenāli," said Thathacharya and proudly exposed the apple.

"I'll go home and prepare for your visit as per the promise," said Tenāli modestly, "come to my house in the afternoon."

In the afternoon, Thathacharya was right at the gates of Tenāli's house.

While entering Tenāli's house, a flash of metal caught Thathacharya's eye and looking up he noted a metal chest lying on the roof of Tenāli's house.

"Tell me honestly," he said to Tenāli, "does that chest over there contain anything valuable?"

"Yes," said Tenāli, "it contains all my money, valuables and most of my wife's ornaments. I thought I had concealed it well. But it has been noticed by you," Tenāli quipped.

"You should've covered it well Tenāli," replied Thathacharya cheerfully, "now though it is outside your house, it is still a part of your house and I can conveniently have a claim over it," said Thathacharya unable to control his excitement.

"First you have to lay your hands on it as per the promise. Remember, it was decided that you may take only one thing from my house with both your hands," remarked Tenāli.

"One is enough," said Thathacharya. Saying this, he went boldly into Tenāli's house, brought out a stout wooden ladder and placed it against the roof.

"Yes, kindly take it down for me," said Tenāli, "and I must thank you for sparing my valuables," exclaimed Tenāli.

"Sparing your valuables?" said Thathacharya, perplexed, "What makes you think I'm going to let you keep your valuables?"

"It was agreed between both of us that the victor would take away only one thing from the house that could be carried out with both his hands," said Tenāli Raman, grinning, "And you have carried out the ladder with both your hands from my house," chuckled Tenāli leaving Thathacharya bewildered.

Life's Lesson

"Do not rush to collect the prize or the reward. Control your enthusiasm. Think through the agreement made. And follow up always in a cool and collected manner. You may spoil the race."

Wise Cracks

- ☼ The important thing about any word is how you understand it. There is a great difference between the right word and the wrong one.
- ☼ The use of a word makes all the difference.
- ☼ Wisdom lies in explaining a word and the one meaning derived from it.

Quotable Nugget

A careless word may kindle strife,
A cruel word may wreck a life;
A bitter word may hate instill,
A brutal word may smile and kill;
A gracious word may smooth the way,
A joyous word may light the day;
A timely word may lessen stress,
"A living word may heal and bless."

        Anonymous.

Hand'some Win

*K*ing Krishnadeva Rāya was the most feared and perfect King. He was a great ruler and a man of justice. He ruled his Kingdom with Dharma on his side.

When the capital city of Hampi witnessed thefts in excess, the King became concerned about the disturbing law and order situation of the Empire. He immediately gave stern orders to Timmarusu, his Mahapradhana (Prime Minister) and the Karyakartha (Chief Secretary) to give 500 lashes publicly to any of the thieves proved guilty. This severe punishment will abstain the culprits from indulging in any such nefarious activity ever again and will also set a lesson for others.

One day, the royal guards caught red handed a group of thieves while they were stealing. The entire group of thieves was produced before the King in the

"Future tense"

Bhuvana Vijayam for punishment.

As the royal guards were to just start giving the punishment with the King's orders, one of the thieves who was rather a clever and quick one, saw a large picture of Lord Venkateswara hanging behind the King. In the picture, the Lord's right hand was raised with an open palm in blessing. Sighting the picture, the clever thief got an idea to claim his forgiveness sympathetically. He said, "O King! How can your men be so ruthless to punish us so harshly when you have the Lord's picture just on your back?"

Hearing the clever thief's remarks, the King paused momentarily. But Tenāli Raman immediately stood up and replied calmly, "That is exactly why the King is asking only for 500 lashes," pointing out at the open hand of the Lord and continued, "The Lord says that the minimum is 5."

The entire court laughed and the thieves were stunned to listen to Tenāli Raman's reply.

Life's Lesson

"The offender always has a right to plead for mercy. The King/Judge always has a right and a duty to disperse fair justice and penalty proportionate to the crime. To fall into the trap of chicanery of the cheat, is only to aggravate the problem."

Wise Cracks

☼ A guilty person should not be allowed to escape.

☼ Even God does not want the guilty to escape the wrath of being punished justly. Punishment is a method to cure a person from misdeeds. The fear of punishment heals up a wicked person.

Quotable Nugget

If punishment reaches not the mind, it hardens the offender.

John Locke

Scene by Scene

Once during the course of deep tete-a-tete, Tenāli Raman said to King Rāya, "Your Honour, telling lies is the most common phenomenon amongst human beings. People always like to lie the moment they get a chance to do so."

"How can you say that Tenāli? I don't agree with you at all. I, being a King, have never lied. There are numerous other instances of people who have never lied," said the King boldly.

"Your Majesty, I hold a point that there is no one in this world who had never lied. Everyone at some or the other instance has lied," said Tenāli self-assuredly.

"Taken for a ride"

"If you are so sure about your opinion, then I challenge you to prove it," the King said.

"Your Majesty, I can prove my assertion provided you reward me suitably," Tenāli asserted.

The King agreed to Tenāli's suggestion.

Saying this Tenāli went away. After that Tenāli was not seen anywhere in the palace for about six months as he was engaged in getting constructed a large and splendid house for himself in the centre of city. He decorated the interiors of his new house colourful and attractive. He got a large mirror affixed to a wall of the house.

When his grand house was ready, Tenāli Raman went to King Rāya's court, disguised himself as a sage beyond recognition. He approached the King and said, "Your Honour, I have built a beautiful house for myself. I pray there regularly. God is very much impressed with my devotion. He is visible in one of the rooms of my house to those people who have never lied in their lives. I request you to feel free to see God for yourself."

King Rāya was eager to visit the sage's house. But to test the sage's words, the King first sent Allasani Peddana (an ashtadiggaja) into the house. Peddana admired the magnificent house. He saw a mirror in the room and his own reflection in that mirror. But he did not see any God as was stated by the sage. Now he was afraid to tell the truth to the King. He came out of the House and lied, "Your Majesty, I saw God in the wall of that sage's house."

But the King was still not very sure. So he sent Nadi Timmanna (another ashtadiggaja) to confirm whether the sage was correct or not. Timmanna also saw his own reflection in the mirror. He was also afraid to tell the truth that he had not seen any God. So he, too, came out and lied to the King, "Oh, Your Majesty! I met God. I am so overwhelmed with emotion to see God."

Now, the King thought, 'I think the sage is correct because two of my ashtadiggajas have also seen God. Let me go in and check the truth myself.'

So the King visited the sage's house and went in. When the King stood before the mirror, he too saw his own reflection. On seeing his own reflection, the King thought, 'According to the sage, only that person who has never lied can see God in the wall. Now if I tell them the truth that I didn't see any God, they will call me a liar.'

So the King went out to the sage and said, "You were right. I have also seen God in the wall."

"Your Majesty, are you sure that you have seen God?" asked the sage.

"Yes, I am sure that I have seen the God," the King replied.

"Did you see God in that wall of the room?" the sage asked again.

The King once again answered positively. When the sage posed the same question once again, the King grew angry and said, "I would have punished you for suspecting me if you were not a holy person."

The sage smiled and pulled off his false beard. He was Tenāli Raman. He said, "Your Majesty, you said that you never lie. Your courtiers are liars and you too behaved like them. Now will you accept that everyone tells a lie sometime or the other."

King Krishnadeva Rāya agreed with him and felt ashamed of his conduct.

LIFE'S LESSON

"Francis Bacon begins his essay on truth with 'what is truth' asked Pilate - and would not want for an answer. Truth and falsehood are with us all the time. To be human is to have both strengths and weaknesses. To deny the weakness is itself a blemish. And not to try and overcome such a weakness, is another blemish."

Wise Cracks

- ☼ We should accept our weaknesses as they are universal facts existing in all. No prejudice has ever been able to prove its case in the court of reason.
- ☼ A prejudice is a vagrant opinion without visible means of support. It is never too late to give up your prejudice.

Quotable Nugget

"Reasoning against a prejudice is like fighting against a shadow; it exhausts the thinker, without visibly affecting the prejudice."

Charles Mildmay

Next is
What

*L*ong before King Krishnadeva Rāya came to the throne of Vijayanagara Empire, the Hindu Kingdoms of Deccan had been repeatedly invaded by the Muslims of North, primarily by Alla-ud-din Khilji and Muhammad-bin-Tughlaq.

During the reign of King Rāya, the Vijayanagara Empire dominated the entire Southern India. The Vijayanagara Empire took strategic steps to shield itself from the onslaughts of Northern Muslim rulers and Deccan Sultanates.

During King Rāya's rule over Vijayanagara, the Dilli Sultanate was led by Babur (Zahir ud-din Muhammad Jala ud-din Babur), the Muslim conqueror from Central Asia who laid the foundation of the Mughal dynasty India.

"Universal identity"

When Babur heard about the ashtadiggajas of King Rāya's Bhuvana Vijayam, especially the talented court jester Tenāli Raman, he expressed his desire to meet Tenāli. Hence, Babur sent his messenger to Hampi to fetch Tenāli Raman. Seeking permission from King Rāya, Tenāli accompanied the messenger to the Dilli Darbar.

The Dilli Sultanate greeted Tenāli and he was given a comfortable stay in the imperial guesthouse. Raman's meeting with the Mughal Emperor was fixed for the next day.

Before the meeting with Tenāli, Emperor Babur had already told his ministers, "I have heard a lot that Tenāli Raman is a distinguished court jester of King Rāya. He has been invited to the Dilli Darbar. He will visit the Royal Court tomorrow. None of you must smile or laugh or appreciate his jokes and witty remarks. I want to test his wisdom as to how he will make us laugh and win a reward?" So the courtiers of Dilli Darbar assured not to smile or laugh or appreciate Tenāli's remarks that day in the court.

Next day, Tenāli Raman arrived at the Dilli Darbar at the scheduled time. Tenāli narrated many witty tales and jokes but neither the courtiers nor the Emperor Babur smiled or laughed or commented at Tenāli's tales. This went on continuously for a fortnight but all remained silent at Tenāli's jokes.

After a fortnight, Tenāli did not go to Dilli Darbar. Rather, he disguised himself and followed Emperor Babur everywhere to note his daily routine.

Tenāli noticed that Emperor Babur used to go regularly for a morning stroll by the river Yamuna with his Prime Minister. On his way, he used to give silver coins to the poor and underprivileged people.

Tenāli followed him and clandestinely observed everything for a few days. Then he drew a plan in his mind.

Next morning, Tenāli Raman disguised himself as an old man. Taking a spade and a mango sapling along with him, Tenāli stood on the banks of river Yamuna waiting for the Emperor to arrive for his morning stroll.

As soon as Tenāli saw the Emperor approaching towards him, he started digging soil with his spade to sow the mango sapling. Emperor Babur noticed the old man planting the mango sapling. He came to the old man and eagerly asked, "May I ask what you are doing, old man?"

"Your Majesty, I have brought this sapling of a very fine variety of mangoes. I'm just sowing the mango sapling," answered the old man earnestly.

"But you are very old and feeble indeed. You won't live long enough to enjoy the fruits of the tree you are planting. Then why are you taking so much trouble at this old age to plant the sapling?" said the Emperor.

"Your Highness, I enjoyed the fruits from the trees planted by my ancestors. The fruits from this tree will be enjoyed and relished by posterity to come. I am not planting this mango tree for myself but for others," the old man quipped.

The Emperor was impressed by the reply of the old man. At once, the Emperor gave a bag full of gold coins to the old man. Receiving the reward from the Emperor, the old man thanked him.

"Your Highness, you are really a kind and thoughtful King. People get the fruits of their labour only when the tree has blossomed but you have given me the fruit of my labour much before. Just the thought of helping others has really benefitted me," said the old man in gratitude.

"I like your humane thoughts, old man. I am really fascinated by your benevolent feelings. You can take this second bag of gold coins also as a reward," Emperor Babur said gently.

"Oh! Your Majesty! Thanks a lot!" the old man said. "This tree will bear fruits only once a year but you have filled my hands with fruits of my labour twice. I am really indebted."

"Once again I like your humanitarian thoughts old man. I am very much pleased to hear such soothing remarks from you. Take this third bag of gold coins as a prize," said the Emperor Babur.

At this, the Prime Minister got concerned. He whispered to Emperor Babur, "Your Majesty, let's leave now. This old man seems to be very intelligent and bright. He will surely claim all the royal wealth from you with his quick and witty remarks."

Emperor Babur laughed aloud and turned to walk away. At this, the old man said, "Your Majesty, can you please care to turn around and just give me a brief look?"

Hearing the old man, Emperor Babur turned around to look and saw Tenāli Raman holding the false beard in his hands. Emperor Babur burst out into laughter on seeing Tenāli.

He said, "Tenāli, I am really impressed. You have very well proved that you are a bright and witty jester. You are a scholar par excellence."

The next day Emperor Babur called Tenāli Raman to the Royal Court and bestowed more rewards on Tenāli Raman. Back to Hampi, King Rāya was happy to know that Tenāli had saved his grace and the splendour of Vijayanagara Empire. The news spread like wild fire.

Life's Lesson

"Innovative thinking - out of the box. Planning to do the unexpected. Meticulous planning and execution. All these are required to win against a well-prepared adversary. It showed Babur, how this can be done. And how this is a lesson for all of us.

Wise Cracks

- ☼ While pride ends in destruction; humility always ends in honour and rewards.
- ☼ The greatest ornaments of an illustrious life are humility and modesty.
- ☼ Humility and modesty are the roots, foundation and bond of all virtues.
- ☼ A humble and modest man is like a good tree, full of fruits and bent low.

Quotable Nugget

A man would adopt humility in order to be or desirable conduct. "Such a man is not discarded anywhere."

Uttaradhyayana Sutra

Handle with Care

One day in the Bhuvana Vijayam, a merchant dressed in all his fineries and carrying a heavy metal box presented himself before King Krishnadeva Rāya. He kept the large box before the King and said, "Your Majesty, I am Guna Shekhar from Bidar. I am a merchant and am going on a pilgrimage to attend the annual Purandaradasa festival in Anegondi. I have kept all my ancestral wealth locked in this metal box. Please keep this box in your safe custody. I will claim it when I return from my journey."

King Rāya agreed to the merchant's request. He called the royal treasurer and after getting the box weighed, the King asked the treasurer to keep the box in safe custody of the royal treasury. But the treasurer told the King about the

"A chip off the old block"

royal treasury being totally full. So the King handed over the metal box to Tenāli Raman for safe custody. Tenāli took the metal box home to keep it safe and ensured all precautions for its safe custody.

A month later, Guna Shekhar returned from his pilgrimage. He went straight to the King's Royal Court to claim his ancestral wealth. The King asked Tenāli to get the box from his house immediately. Tenāli went home to get the box.

When Tenāli reached his home and lifted the metal box, he was shocked. The box weighed too less than its weight when it was weighed for the first time. Tenāli understood now that Guna Shekhar had tried to cheat the King.

Tenāli observed the metal box minutely for sometime. Then he hurriedly reached the Royal Court. In a fearful tone, he addressed the King with folded hands, "Your Majesty, the ancestors of this merchant have forced themselves into my house. They are not letting me bring the box here."

The merchant roared in anger, "He is a wicked person, Your Majesty. He wants to lay claim on the wealth of my fathers and forefathers."

The King said, "Tenāli, we all will go to your house right now. If you are proved a liar, then you will have to face severe punishment."

So the King and a few courtiers alongwith Guna Shekhar went to Tenāli's house. Tenāli led them to the room where he had kept the box.

There the King and the courtiers saw that a large number of ants were going in and out of the metal box. Seeing this, the King immediately ordered the attendants to open the box. To the utter amazement of all those present, they found jaggery (gur) stored in the metal box. More than half of the jaggery had already been eaten up by the ants. Everybody understood Guna Shekhar's malicious scheme to deceive the King and the innocent Tenāli Raman.

The King and the courtiers were taken aback to see the merchant's evil plan to cheat the King. The King immediately ordered the merchant's arrest.

Life's Lesson

"Always look for the little indicators. They are generally missed. Yet, they make the big difference and help to take the right and final decisions. It requires a sharp eye, sound hearing and an astute mind. Finally, it may 'be simple my dear Watson'(Holmes) except that it is not that simple."

Wise Cracks

☼ The first step towards wisdom is scepticism (doubt). Never take anything for granted.

☼ Scepticism is the chastity of the intellect. Believe nothing without reason and be on your guard against everything. When a man tells you that he's going to put all his cards on the table, you always look up his sleeves.

Quotable Nugget

"I think one of the troubles of the world has been the habit of dogmatically believing something or other... we ought always to entertain our opinions with some measure of doubt."

Bertrand Russell

Discovery
Lesson

*H*anumantha Rao, an elderly friendly man lived alone in a village on the outskirts of Hampi. He was a close friend of Tenāli Raman.

Hanumantha was liked by all villagers who would often come over to his house and express their sympathy that his only son had gone far away to Chandragiri for studies. They wondered aloud if his son would ever return. To all their concern, Hanumantha also felt upset for his son studying far away. But Tenāli would always say to Hanumantha, "Everything happens for the good."

This annoyed Hanumantha a lot and he every time demanded justification from Tenāli for making such a prompt and elusive statement. Tenāli always

"Everything happens just for the good"

assured that whenever appropriate time will come, Hanumantha will himself understand what Tenāli meant by making such a statement.

One day, Hanumantha's son returned to his village. The entire village was very happy for Hanumantha and all villagers came over to congratulate him. Tenāli also came and like always, he said politely, "Everything happens for the good."

Barely a few days had passed, when one day Hanumantha's son fell off a horse's back miserably and broke his leg. Once again the entire village came over to Hanumantha's house to express their concern. Tenāli also came to console and once again said compassionately, "Everything happens for the good." At such a critical occasion, the villagers were surprised to hear this from Tenāli. Hanumantha was also annoyed to hear Tenāli's statement at that moment when his son was crying in pain. Hanumantha wondered that Tenāli might be making a mockery of his sorrow and thought what good could be there in the broken leg of his son.

A few days later, the Dandanayaka (royal army commander) came to the village and enrolled all active young men into the royal army as Kavalus (royal guards) in the wake of fierce invasions of the Bahmani Sultanate. When the Dandanayaka and Rajya Adhikaris (imperial officers) came to Hanumantha Rao's house, they found his son with a broken leg, so they left him behind.

Once again, all the villagers came to Hanumantha's house to congratulate him for his good luck. Tenāli also came and like always showing his concern said, "Everything happens for the good."

Hanumantha listening to Tenāli's statement immediately understood the real essence of Tenāli's always making this statement and felt reassured. He knew that his son will remain with him and that broken leg was a boon in disguise.

Life's Lesson

There is tide in the affairs of men, which taken at the flood, lead on.... yes, there is a certain destiny - God's plan, which makes the adage relevant 'Work as if everything depended on you - Pray as if everything depended on God.'

Wise Cracks

- ☼ Life is a great school in which you constantly learn how to plan and work better and achieve better and greater things.

- ☼ Every man's life is a plan of God which goes at its own pace, at its own will and own direction.

- ☼ Life is not 'having and getting', but in 'being and becoming'.

- ☼ Laws of nature and life can't be changed but only accepted.

- ☼ Nature can't be governed but can only be obeyed.

Quotable Nugget

Nature creates ability; luck provides it with opportunity.

Anonymous

☼☼☼

Adieu to Raman

One morning, while Tenāli Raman was taking his usual stroll in the garden, a poisonous snake bit him. The fatal venom immediately spread all over his body.

Distinguished physicians were called to cure Tenāli's snake bite. But none of the treatments worked despite best efforts. Tenāli lay haplessly on the death bed in acute pain. As a last wish, Tenāli desired to meet His Highness, King Krishnadeva Rāya.

Soon, a messenger was sent to the Royal Court to convey the King that Tenāli lay breathing his last and before dying he wishes to see the King.

"Friends forever"

The King wouldn't believe the messenger. In fact, he thought that Tenāli was again upto some mischief and playing another of his tricks. He told the messenger, "Tenāli is very clever but he can't trick me anymore. Tell him to quit his death ploy and attend the Bhuvana Vijayam."

The messenger insisted that it was not Tenāli's naughtiness but in fact he was bitten by a deadly snake and may die any moment. But the King was not convinced.

The messenger returned to Tenāli and narrated him the entire episode. This episode brought tears to the eyes of Tenāli. He wept, "What a mockery! No one believes a jester. A jester is only believed for his pranks, tricks, tomfoolery and monkey business. I am sure that when the King comes to know of my demise, he will be utterly sad. But I am glad that all through my life I have always endeavoured to serve the King with loyalty. I can now die with full satisfaction."

With these distressing words, Tenāli died with a smile on his face.

Later, when the King gave a second thought to the messenger's remarks and his (messenger's) remorseful face, he (King) held that perhaps the messenger was telling truth. So the King decided to pay a visit to Tenāli's house.

When the King entered Tenāli's house, it was already too late. Tenāli lay dead. There was gloom everywhere, and his family members were wailing around the dead body.

That sight traumatised the King. He moved close to Tenāli's corpse and cried in agony, "Tenāli! Stop that dead act! You can't leave us like that! We know you are deceiving us. Please get up! If you get up, I will give you all my wealth in reward."

The King started crying with tears rolling down his cheeks. The courtiers tried to console the King and took him to the Palace. The King Rāya was totally shattered and announced state mourning.

Next day, state funeral with full honour was given to Tenāli. Lakhs paid homage at the funeral. Holy fire was lit to the pyre. Hymns were chanted. Flames leapt up. People cried and wailed. The entire Vijayanagara Empire moaned. Even Tenāli's enemies sobbed. A column of smoke rose from the pyre towards the boundless sky. The King tearfully witnessed it disappearing into the sky wondering, "The Vikatakavi has today left me alone. There will never be a witty and intelligent jester like Tenāli Raman ever again."

Life's Lesson

"Crying wolf has its attendant problems. A loss of crediility. No one believes when the wolf actually comes visiting.

And satisfaction of a job well done has its own rewards, even if there is neither time or opportunity to acknowledge such satisfaction."

Wise Cracks

- ☼ A really great man is broadly known by three signs : kindness, humanity and moderation.
- ☼ Some of us are born great, some achieve greatness and some have greatness thrust upon them.
- ☼ One thing is sure that the world cannot do without great men and the death of a great mind is a catastrophe.

Quotable Nugget

"Immortality is when a man dies but his words live on in man."

Samuel Butler

Books Miscellaneous from the same Publication

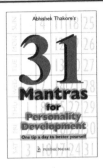

31 Mantras for Personality Development

- Abhishek Thakore

31 practical tips and techniques in this book will teach you how to live each moment, each hour and each day to the fullest. By the simple expedient of mantras, the book takes you one step closer to becoming a better, more successful, happy and contented human being.

Unlike other books on personality development and happiness, which are seemingly practical but not practicable, these steps can transform you into a new person within 31 days.

All you have to do is read and practise just one tip everyday...beginning NOW!

And within a month, there will be a New You.

pages 104, price Rs.88/-

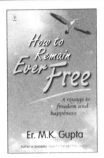

How to Remain Ever Free

- Er. M.K. Gupta

In this book, the author makes a clear distinction between real freedom and the so-called casual freedom of doing anything as per one's whims and fancies.

This book is divided into small chapters, with eye-catching illustrations to avoid monotony while reading.

Further, you can start reading the book from anywhere as every chapter is independent and complete in itself.

This book has a vibe and style of its own which makes it completely different from the other books of this category.

pages 208, price Rs.96/-

Books Miscellaneous from the same Publication

Can is the Word of Power

– Barendra Kumar

Can is...Power not only advocates the same, but also covers all the aspects of personal growth – spiritual, emotional, physical, mental, and inspires to make a successful career to build a meaningful life. Needless to say, it is equally useful for average to excelling students, as well as their custodians/well-wishers.

This book, for self-analysis, improvement and success, with hundreds of inspirational quotes and hints of stories of different event-makers, from different countries – past and present – to expand the databank, will surely induce success thinking for better personal life, yielding to greater national living.

pages 292, price Rs.150/-

Secrets of Leadership

– Luis S. R. Vas
& Anita S. R. Vas

The Panchatantra is a work relevant for all times, whether it is used in a management workshop or as a general guide to daily living. Leadership is involved in both.

In this collection, the authors have tried to show what bearing these fables have on their leadership skills. They have highlighted some of the morals embedded in the fables themselves as well as provided modern insights at the end of each story.

In the conclusion, the authors have stated the five leadership secrets of the Panchatantra as revealed in the five tantras and combined them with a typical modern management plan designed to bring the readers' newly-learnt leadership skills to fruition.

pages 136, price Rs.96/-

Books Miscellaneous from the same Publication

Solve Your Problems – The Birbal Way

– Luis S. R. Vas

Unravelling in the Court of Akbar, the well-known Birbal stories illustrate the minister's sagacity and problem-solving acumen. The author thought it would be appropriate to unveil the managerial wisdom and problem-solving principles that Birbal's stories embody.

They have retold some of the Birbal stories that they gathered and at the end of each they have pointed out the management moral of the narrative, whose wisdom remains as fresh as ever. They have divided each story into two parts. The first part consists of the problem; the second part provides Birbal's solution.

pages 200, price Rs.110/-

100 Minutes That'll change The Way You Live

– Dr. L. Prakash

Real life, at times, tends to get mundane and boring.

How to survive against such inertia and overwhelming odds in life is the *mool* mantra of this unique little book. These 'top tips' will help you live life more peacefully and more successfully, irrespective of whether you are young or old, man or woman, businessman or executive, professional or in service.

This is real stuff for real people, no lectures, no empty talk, only immensely practical wisdom! That too told in a humorous way by the author who has himself learnt them in the process of surviving some great crises in life, and thus speaks with the authority of personal experience.

pages 127, price Rs.135/-

Books Miscellaneous from the same Publication

365 Recipes That will Make You Think Positive

– Alan Cohen

Blind living makes the journey of life arduous and tiresome. Guidance from an enlightened person makes the life pleasant, enjoyable and fleeting.

This book contains 365+ enlightened thoughts for each day of the year that could help you start your day on a positive note. At the end of the day, the book will help you review your day in light of these principles.

By applying the principles contained within these pages, there will be tremendous healing, inspiration and positive changes in your life.

pages 366, price Rs.175/-

Better Management & Effective Leadership

– Narayanji Misra

This book, Better Management and Effective Leadership through the Indian Scriptures, aims at discovering the treasure hidden in the Indian texts, making the management scholars all over the world feel proud of our literary heritage and appreciate the farsightedness of the Indian thinkers.

It is an endeavour to reveal that, be it in any sphere of academics, Indian scholars were in no way secondary to their western counterparts; they were rather the precursors.

pages 207, price Rs.225/-

Books Miscellaneous from the same Publication

Indian Saints & Sages

– Prof. Shrikant Prasoon

Indian Saints and Sages presents in short the celestial power, and miraculous and supernatural wonders related to numerous Saints who were enlightened and brilliant persons with blissful souls. Their appearance was divine and the departure sublime. Most of them took *Samadhi* alive and in the presence of many; some entered the caves and never returned back, some changed into blazing light and some became flowers.

The book tells how the God came to eat from the hands of devotees, played with them, listened to their discourses and hymns and fulfilled their simple, general, esoteric and extraordinary desires.

pages 268, price Rs.150/-

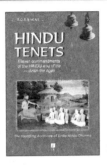

Hindu Tenets

– J AGARWAL

This book lists the eleven principles on which the Vedic Hindu Dharma rests till today. They may be called the Eleven Tenets — the founding doctrines of Hinduism — that give the entire picture in a very concise form.

The most significant among them are: belief in one Supreme Being, in His revealed wisdom in the shape of the Vedas; in the great law of karma or action; in the theory of reincarnation of the soul; and belief in the legacy of the great rishis of the bygone days, who are the guiding force in the lives of Indians even today.

pages 152, price Rs.150/-

Books Miscellaneous from the same Publication

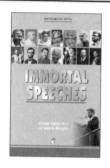

Pearls of Spiritual Wisdom

– Dr. Aparna Chattopadhyay

Living in spirituality has therapeutic value, as the latest medical research reveals. When sound in spirituality, you become less prone to emotional and physical disorders, since your inner system is fortified and better attuned to withstand the tensions of present-day living.

Make spiritual ideals a practical part of daily living for success, happiness and bliss to be your handmaidens forever.

Go for this practical guide to everyday spirituality and empower yourself by contemplating and comprehending the basic truths of life.

pages 160, price Rs.80/-

Immortal Speeches

– Harshvardhan Dutt

Immortal Speeches is a thoughtful compilation by Harshvardhan Dutta which consists of inspiring and dynamic speeches by world-famous orators.

This book contains Indian (**Mahatma Gandhi, Nehru, Bal Gangadhar Tilak, Netaji Subhash Chandra Bose, Lala Lajpat Rai,** etc.) as well as world renowned speakers (**Winston Churchill, Roosevelt, Kennedy, Dr. Martin Luther King, Lincoln, Stalin,** etc.) who have delivered some memorable speeches.

And as an additional bonus acts as a practical guide for preparing speeches, timeless features of speeches, body language and classification of speeches, etc.

pages 135, price Rs.80/-